We have designed this guide with both Foundation and Higher candidates in mind. It includes:

- Foundation material in BLUE.

- Higher material in GREEN.

- Grammar sections in RED, integrated into the main section of the booklet so that you can see how the points that we cover apply to a particular topic.

- A mini-test at regular intervals to enable you to assess how your revision is going.

- A section on exam technique.

- A grammar summary.

  The guide is intended for use with any GCSE syllabus.

CONSULTANT EDITORS ...

- **Debbie Hill** - Former Head of Modern Languages at Magdalen College School, Brackley.

- **Gaynor Garton** - Teacher of Modern Languages at Ousedale School, Newport Pagnell.

CONTENTS

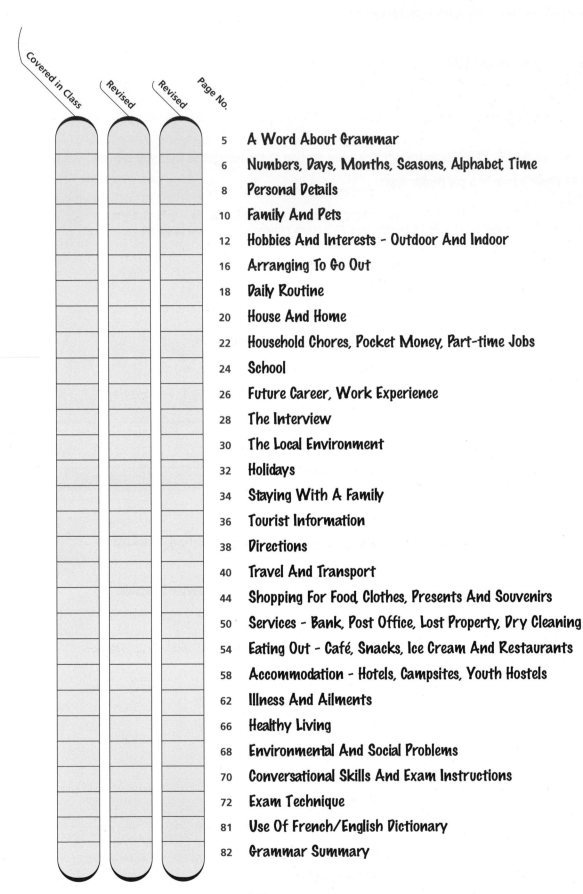

GRAMMAR CONTENTS

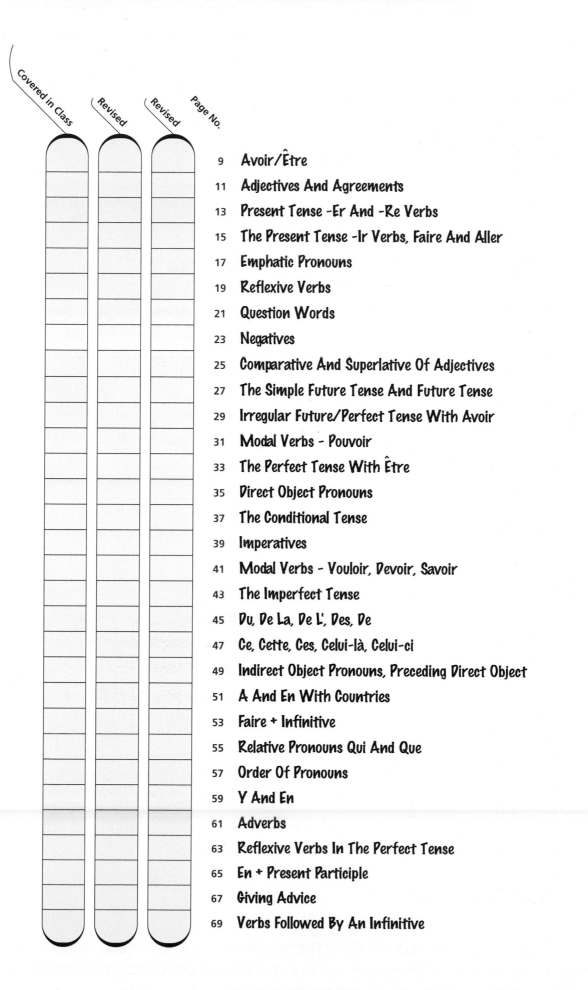

This guide is intended to consolidate what you have learnt throughout your course and to refresh your memory as you approach your exams.

- Use our mini-tests to constantly test yourself ... WITHOUT LOOKING AT THE BOOK!

- Don't just read, learn actively! Talk to yourself in French, record yourself, work with a friend, write things down.

- When you have revised a section, tick the boxes on the content page, this will help you to see how your revision is progressing.

- Jot down anything which will help you to remember, no matter how trivial.

- Remember that our vocabulary lists don't include everything. Use your dictionary to add to them.

- Remember that if you are entered for different levels in the different skills you will need to use both Foundation and Higher level material.

Grammar

To get a good **GCSE** grade you must have a sound understanding of the rules of French grammar, and be able to apply these rules in your own spoken and written French. Throughout this guide we have tried to show you points of grammar in the context of a particular topic. Where this has not been possible, grammar points have been included in the grammar summary on pages 82 - 94.

You will need to know the following grammatical terms:

1. <u>Noun</u> - the name of an object or person or place

    eg.   le crayon, la soeur, la France

2. <u>Singular and Plural</u> - a singular noun means there is only one thing or person, a plural noun means there is more than one

    eg.   singular le chat, l'arbre

    plural les chats, les arbres

3. <u>Pronoun</u> - used in place of a noun

    eg.   la fille sourit. <u>Elle</u> sourit (<u>Elle</u> (she) is the pronoun replacing la fille.)

4. <u>Adjective</u> - a "describing" word, giving more information about a noun

    eg.   un chat <u>noir</u>, les cheveux <u>blonds</u>

5. <u>Verb</u> - a "doing" word, indicating the actions of people or things

    eg.   il <u>joue</u> au tennis

6. <u>Subject</u> - of a verb is the person or thing "doing the verb"

    eg.   <u>Je</u> mange une pomme (<u>Je</u> is the subject of the verb.)

7. <u>Direct Object</u> - of a verb is the person or thing which is having something done to it

    eg.   Je mange <u>une pomme</u> (<u>une pomme</u> is the direct object of the verb.)

8. <u>Indirect Object</u> - of a verb usually has "to" or "for" in front of it; (in French, à, au or aux)

    eg.   Je vais donner ce livre <u>à mon frère</u> ("ce livre" is the direct object, and "mon frère" the indirect object of the verb "donner")

9. <u>Infinitive</u> - the form of the verb found in the dictionary meaning "<u>to do</u> something"

    eg.   jouer (<u>to</u> play); vendre (<u>to</u> sell); choisir (<u>to</u> choose)

10. <u>Tense</u> - of a verb tells you <u>when</u> the action takes place - in the past, present or future

11. <u>Adverb</u> - describes a verb, often explains "how", "when" or "where"

    eg.   elle parle <u>lentement</u>

12. <u>Preposition</u> - describes the position of a person or thing

    eg.   <u>devant</u> le cinéma

Foundation

0	- zéro	21	- vingt et un	90	- quatre-vingt-dix
1	- un	22	- vingt-deux	91	- quatre-vingt-onze
2	- deux	23	- vingt-trois	99	- quatre-vingt-dix-neuf
3	- trois	24	- vingt-quatre	100	- cent
4	- quatre	25	- vingt-cinq	101	- cent un
5	- cinq	26	- vingt-six	110	- cent dix
6	- six	27	- vingt-sept	200	- deux cents
7	- sept	28	- vingt-huit	201	- deux cent un
8	- huit	29	- vingt-neuf	221	- deux cent vingt et un
9	- neuf	30	- trente	1,000	- mille
10	- dix	31	- trente et un	1,200	- mille deux cents
11	- onze	40	- quarante	1,202	- mille deux cent deux
12	- douze	50	- cinquante	2,000	- deux mille
13	- treize	60	- soixante	1,000,000	- un million
14	- quatorze	70	- soixante-dix	1,000,000,000	- un milliard
15	- quinze	71	- soixante et onze		
16	- seize	72	- soixante-douze		
17	- dix-sept	73	- soixante-treize		
18	- dix-huit	79	- soixante-dix-neuf		
19	- dix-neuf	80	- quatre-vingts		
20	- vingt	81	- quatre-vingt-un		

Remember: to pay attention to those numbers linked by - or by et, and whether there is an 's' on the end.

In order to change 2 into 2nd add (ième) to the number.

deux + ième = deuxième (second)
trois + ième = troisième (third)
quatre + ième = quatrième (fourth) (drop final 'e' from quatre).
BUT un (one) = premier/première (f) (first)

Vocabulary

Les jours de la semaine – Days of the week

lundi	-	Monday
mardi	-	Tuesday
mercredi	-	Wednesday
jeudi	-	Thursday
vendredi	-	Friday
samedi	-	Saturday
dimanche	-	Sunday

Les mois de l'année – Months of the year

janvier	-	January	juillet	-	July
février	-	February	août	-	August
mars	-	March	septembre	-	September
avril	-	April	octobre	-	October
mai	-	May	novembre	-	November
juin	-	June	décembre	-	December

Both days of the week and months of the year are written with a small letter in French.

mercredi	-	Wednesday, <u>on</u> Wednesday
<u>le</u> mercredi	-	on Wednesday<u>s</u>

<u>en</u> janvier, - <u>in</u> January
or <u>au</u> mois <u>de</u> janvier

Les Saisons – The Seasons

Le printemps	-	Spring
L'été	-	Summer
L'automne	-	Autumn
L'hiver	-	Winter
en été	-	in Summer
en automne	-	in Autumn
en hiver	-	in Winter
BUT au printemps	-	in Spring

La date – The date

le quatorze janvier	-	14th January
le vingt-six mars	-	26th March
BUT le premier août	-	1st August

Foundation

It is useful to know the alphabet in French; you may be required to spell something (usually your name) in the oral exam or to listen to a word being spelt.

as in cat	say	as in ugh	as in j'ai	ee	Ka	em		oh	koo	es	as in Hugh	double vay	ee grek
A	**B** **C**	**D**	**E** **F**	**G**	**H** **I** **J**	**K** **L**	**M** **N**	**O**	**P** **Q**	**R**	**S** **T** **U**	**V** **W**	**X** **Y** **Z**
bay	day	et	ash	as in j'y	el	en	pay	air	tay	vay	ix	zed

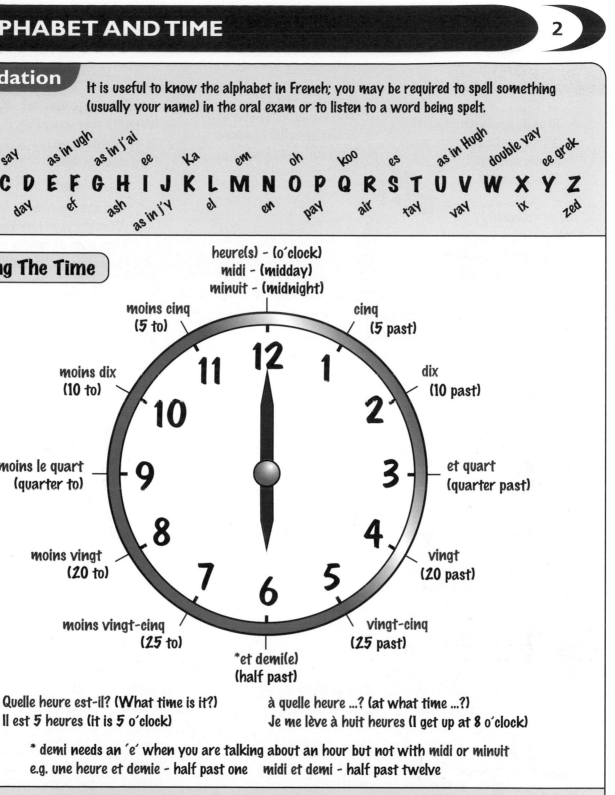

Telling The Time

heure(s) - (o'clock)
midi - (midday)
minuit - (midnight)

moins cinq (5 to)
cinq (5 past)
moins dix (10 to)
dix (10 past)
moins le quart (quarter to)
et quart (quarter past)
moins vingt (20 to)
vingt (20 past)
moins vingt-cinq (25 to)
vingt-cinq (25 past)
*et demi(e) (half past)

Quelle heure est-il? (What time is it?)   à quelle heure ...? (at what time ...?)
Il est 5 heures (it is 5 o'clock)   Je me lève à huit heures (I get up at 8 o'clock)

* demi needs an 'e' when you are talking about an hour but not with midi or minuit
e.g. une heure et demie - half past one   midi et demi - half past twelve

---

You will also need to be able to understand and use the 24 hour clock.

a.m.

	0.10	Il est zéro heures dix
	1.00	Il est une heure
	2.15	Il est deux heures quinze
	5.30	Il est cinq heures trente
	9.45	Il est neuf heures quarante-cinq

p.m.

	12.10	Il est douze heures dix
	13.00	Il est treize heures
	14.15	Il est quatorze heures quinze
	17.30	Il est dix-sept heures trente
	21.45	Il est vingt et une heures quarante-cinq

Foundation

Tu es de quelle nationalité?
(What nationality are you?)
Je suis anglais(e).
(I am English.)

Tu peux te décrire?
(Can you describe yourself?)
Je suis grand(e) et mince.
(I am tall and slim.)

Comment t'appelles-tu?
(What is your name?)
Je m'appelle Jane.
(My name is Jane.)

Où es-tu né(e)?
Where were you born?
Je suis né(e) à Londres.
(I was born in London.)

Quel est ton nom de famille?
(What is your surname?)
Mon nom de famille est Smith.
(My surname is Smith.)

Quel est ton numéro de téléphone?
(What is your telephone number?)
C'est le 264508 (vingt-six quarante-cinq zéro huit)
(It's 264508.)

Comment ça s'écrit?
(How do you spell it?)
Ça s'écrit S-M-I-T-H.
(It is spelt S-M-I-T-H.)

Quel âge as-tu?
(How old are you?)
J'ai quinze (15) ans.
(I'm 15 years old.)

Quelle est ton adresse?
(What's your address?)
J'habite numéro 20 Primula Close, Northampton.
(I live at 20 Primula Close, Northampton).

Quelle est la date de ton anniversaire?
(When is your birthday?)
C'est le 28 mai.
(It's on the 28th May.)

Où habites-tu?
(Where do you live?)
J'habite (à) Newport Pagnell.
(I live in Newport Pagnell.)

Vocabulary

date de naissance	-	date of birth
lieu de naissance	-	place of birth
domicile	-	address
état civil	-	marital status
célibataire	-	single
marié(e)	-	married
séparé(e)	-	separated
divorcé(e)	-	divorced
métier	-	profession
étudiant(e)	-	student
écossais(e)	-	Scottish
irlandais(e)	-	Irish
gallois(e)	-	Welsh
britannique	-	British
la religion	-	religon
catholique	-	catholic
protestant(e)	-	protestant
musulman(e)	-	muslim
hindou(e)	-	hindu
juif (ive)	-	jewish

grand(e)	-	tall
petit(e)	-	small/short
de taille moyenne	-	medium
court(e)	-	short (hair)
long(ue)	-	long
frisé(e)	-	wavy
bouclé(e)	-	curly
raid(e)	-	straight
roux	-	auburn
noir(e)	-	black
blond(e)	-	blond
châtain	-	light brown
mince	-	slim
joli(e)	-	pretty
laid(e)	-	ugly

(feminine forms given in brackets)

Remember:
J'ai les yeux gris = I have grey eyes
J'ai les cheveux blonds = I have blond hair

Higher

At Higher Level you need to include language that is more complex and aim for greater accuracy, fluency and variety of vocabulary. Here are some ideas to help you extend your language:

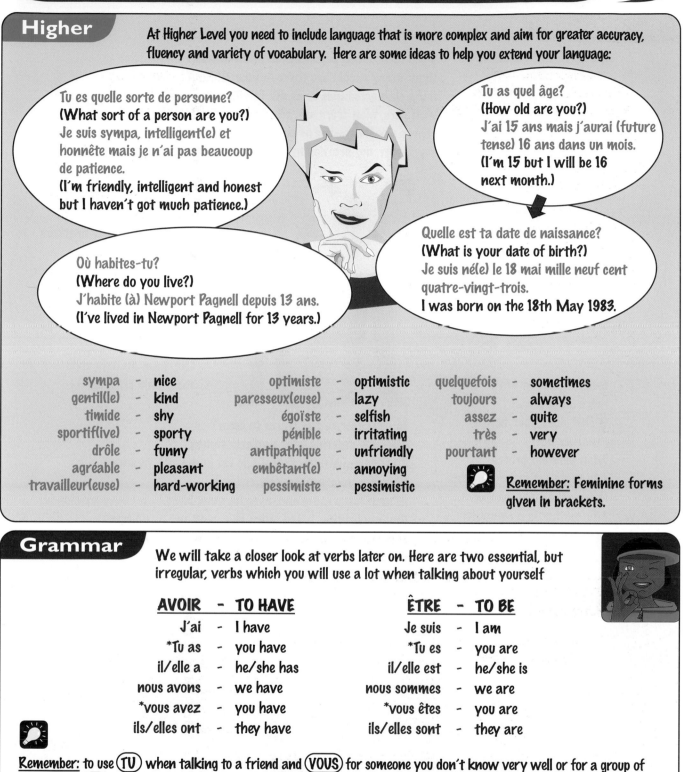

Tu es quelle sorte de personne?
(What sort of a person are you?)
Je suis sympa, intelligent(e) et honnête mais je n'ai pas beaucoup de patience.
(I'm friendly, intelligent and honest but I haven't got much patience.)

Tu as quel âge?
(How old are you?)
J'ai 15 ans mais j'aurai (future tense) 16 ans dans un mois.
(I'm 15 but I will be 16 next month.)

Où habites-tu?
(Where do you live?)
J'habite (à) Newport Pagnell depuis 13 ans.
(I've lived in Newport Pagnell for 13 years.)

Quelle est ta date de naissance?
(What is your date of birth?)
Je suis né(e) le 18 mai mille neuf cent quatre-vingt-trois.
I was born on the 18th May 1983.

sympa	-	nice	optimiste	-	optimistic	quelquefois	-	sometimes
gentil(le)	-	kind	paresseux(euse)	-	lazy	toujours	-	always
timide	-	shy	égoïste	-	selfish	assez	-	quite
sportif(ive)	-	sporty	pénible	-	irritating	très	-	very
drôle	-	funny	antipathique	-	unfriendly	pourtant	-	however
agréable	-	pleasant	embêtant(e)	-	annoying			
travailleur(euse)	-	hard-working	pessimiste	-	pessimistic			

Remember: Feminine forms given in brackets.

Grammar

We will take a closer look at verbs later on. Here are two essential, but irregular, verbs which you will use a lot when talking about yourself

AVOIR	–	**TO HAVE**		**ÊTRE**	–	**TO BE**
J'ai	-	I have		Je suis	-	I am
*Tu as	-	you have		*Tu es	-	you are
il/elle a	-	he/she has		il/elle est	-	he/she is
nous avons	-	we have		nous sommes	-	we are
*vous avez	-	you have		*vous êtes	-	you are
ils/elles ont	-	they have		ils/elles sont	-	they are

Remember: to use (TU) when talking to a friend and (VOUS) for someone you don't know very well or for a group of people. Also (ILS) (they) can refer to a group of males, or a **MIXED** group of males and females.

Mini Test

It is important to check regularly that you have absorbed the vocabulary and phrases from each section. Here are a few tasks for this section:

1. Say as much as you can about yourself in French, without looking at this guide. Record it onto cassette and time yourself.

2. Play back the tape and see if you can correct your own mistakes.

3. Refer back to the guide and add **5** more details.

4. Practise form-filling. Write out the various headings and without reference to the guide, fill in the form.

Foundation

Il y a combien de personnes dans ta famille?
(How many people are there in your family?)
Il y a cinq personnes dans ma famille - ma mère,
mon père, mon frère, ma sœur et moi.
(There are five people in my family - my mother,
my father, my brother, my sister and myself.)

Tu as un animal?
Tu peux le décrire?
(Have you got a pet?
Can you describe it?)
J'ai un chat. Il s'appelle
Bobby. Il est noir
et blanc. Il est mignon.
(I have a cat. His name
is Bobby. He is black
and white.
He is sweet.)

Tu as des frères ou
des sœurs?
(Have you got any brothers
or sisters?)
Oui, j'ai un frère et une sœur.
(Yes, I have one brother and
one sister.)
Non, je suis fils unique/fille
unique.
(No, I am an only child
(boy) only child (girl).)

Que fait ton père/ta
mère dans la vie?
(What does your father
/mother do?)
Mon père est professeur.
Ma mère est programmeuse.
(My father is a teacher.
My mother is a computer
programmer.)

Tu peux décrire ton frère/ta sœur?
(Can you describe your brother/sister?)
Il est comment, ton frère? Elle est comment, ta sœur?
(What is your brother/sister like?)
Il/mon frère est grand, avec les yeux bleus et les cheveux blonds.
(He/my brother is tall, with blue eyes and blond hair.)
Elle/ma sœur est petite, avec les yeux gris et les cheveux
marron. Elle est mince.
(She/my sister is small, with grey eyes and
brown hair. She is slim.)

See page 26 for list of professions.

Vocabulary

La Famille	-	The Family
le père	-	father
la mère	-	mother
les parents	-	parents
le grand-père	-	grandfather
la grand-mère	-	grandmother
les grands-parents	-	grandparents
le petit-fils	-	grandson
la petite-fille	-	granddaughter
les petits-enfants	-	grandchildren
l'oncle	-	uncle
la tante	-	aunt
le neveu	-	nephew
la nièce	-	niece
le cousin	-	cousin (m)
la cousine	-	cousin (f)
l'enfant	-	child
le bébé	-	baby

Les animaux	-	pets
le chien	-	dog
le chat	-	cat
le cheval	-	horse
le lapin	-	rabbit
l'oiseau	-	bird
le hamster	-	hamster
le cochon d'Inde	-	guinea pig
le poisson rouge	-	goldfish
la tortue	-	tortoise
la souris	-	mouse

Remember:
Je n'ai pas d'animaux - I haven't got any pets
il/elle a les yeux bleus/ les cheveux frisés/
une barbe/ une moustache. (he/she has blue eyes/
wavy hair/ a beard/ a moustache.)
il/elle porte des lunettes - (he/she wears glasses.)

Higher

Tu t'entends bien avec ton père/
ta mère/ton frère etc?
**Do you get on well with your
father/mother/brother etc?**
Oui, je m'entends bien avec lui/elle.
Yes, I get on well with him/her.
Ça dépend. Quelquefois il/elle
est trop stricte.
**That depends. Sometimes
he/she is too strict.**

Parle-moi un peu de ta famille.
(Tell me a bit about your family.)
Nous sommes cinq; mon père, ma mère,
mon frère, ma soeur et moi.
**There are five of us; my father,
my mother, my brother,
my sister and me.**

Il/elle est comment de caractère?
What sort of person is he/she?
Il/elle est marrant(e) et travailleur(euse).
He/she is funny and hardworking.

Tu ressembles à ton père/ta mère?
Do you look like your father/mother?
Oui, nous nous ressemblons beaucoup/un peu.
Yes, we look a lot/a little alike.
Non, nous ne nous ressemblons pas du tout.
No, we don't look at all alike.

Grammar

Adjectives with Agreements

An adjective is a DESCRIBING word e.g. grand, rouge, mince. All adjectives in French must "agree" with the noun (the object being described), depending on whether the noun is masculine, feminine, singular or plural. The pattern for regular adjectives is as follows:

Masculine	Feminine	Masculine Plural	Feminine Plural
grand	grande	grands	grandes
bleu	bleue	bleus	bleues

e.g. Mon père est grand avec les yeux (masculine plural) bleus.
Ma mère est petite.
Mes soeurs (feminine plural) sont grandes.

If the adjective already ends in -e or -s, no extra -e or -s is added.

gris	grise	gris	grises
mince	mince	minces	minces

The feminine form of some adjectives is irregular.

e.g.

blanc	blanche
gros	grosse
sportif	sportive

For more information on adjectives, see Grammar Summary page 83 - 85.

A good dictionary will supply the feminine form of an adjective if it is irregular.

Marron (brown) is an INVARIABLE adjective. This means it does not change, no matter what it is describing.

un pantalon marron - brown trousers
une robe marron - a brown dress
les yeux marron - brown eyes

When using clair (light) and foncé (dark) with a colour, both adjectives are invariable.

e.g.

J'ai les yeux bleu clair - I've got light blue eyes
J'ai les yeux brun foncé - I've got dark brown eyes

Foundation

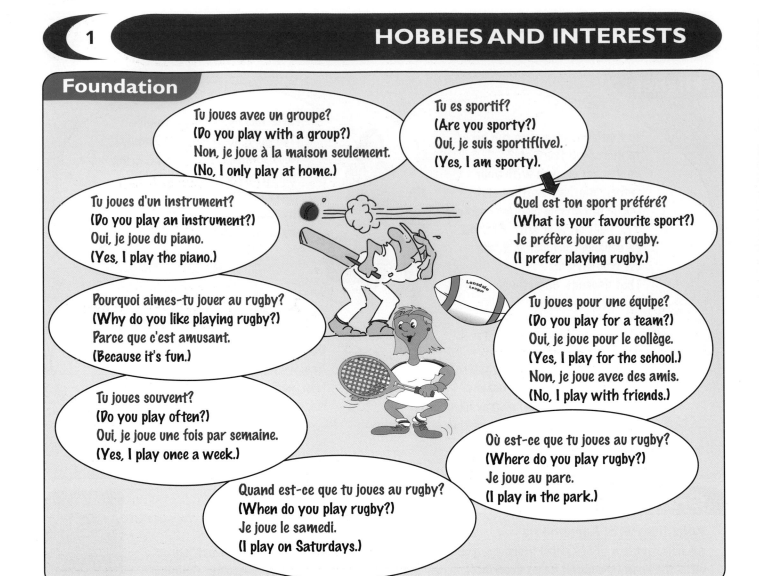

Tu joues avec un groupe?
(Do you play with a group?)
Non, je joue à la maison seulement.
(No, I only play at home.)

Tu es sportif?
(Are you sporty?)
Oui, je suis sportif(ive).
(Yes, I am sporty).

Tu joues d'un instrument?
(Do you play an instrument?)
Oui, je joue du piano.
(Yes, I play the piano.)

Quel est ton sport préféré?
(What is your favourite sport?)
Je préfère jouer au rugby.
(I prefer playing rugby.)

Pourquoi aimes-tu jouer au rugby?
(Why do you like playing rugby?)
Parce que c'est amusant.
(Because it's fun.)

Tu joues pour une équipe?
(Do you play for a team?)
Oui, je joue pour le collège.
(Yes, I play for the school.)
Non, je joue avec des amis.
(No, I play with friends.)

Tu joues souvent?
(Do you play often?)
Oui, je joue une fois par semaine.
(Yes, I play once a week.)

Où est-ce que tu joues au rugby?
(Where do you play rugby?)
Je joue au parc.
(I play in the park.)

Quand est-ce que tu joues au rugby?
(When do you play rugby?)
Je joue le samedi.
(I play on Saturdays.)

Vocabulary

Jouer	-	to play	le stade	-	the stadium
au tennis	-	tennis	le terrain de sport	-	the sports ground
au football	-	football	le parc	-	the park
au cricket	-	cricket	le collège	-	school
au rugby	-	rugby	le club des jeunes	-	the youth club
au netball	-	netball	la piscine	-	the swimming pool
au basket-ball	-	basketball	la patinoire	-	skating rink
au ping-pong	-	table tennis	au cinéma	-	at the cinema
au baby-foot	-	table football	au théâtre	-	at the theatre
aux échecs	-	chess	seul(e)	-	alone
aux cartes	-	cards	avec mes copains	-	with my friends
du piano	-	the piano	avec un groupe scolaire	-	with a group from school
du violon	-	violin	dans un orchestre	-	in an orchestra
de la guitare	-	guitar	dans une bande	-	in a band
de la flûte	-	flute	dans une équipe	-	in a team
de la flûte à bec	-	recorder	souvent	-	often
de la batterie	-	drums	de temps en temps	-	from time to time
de la trompette	-	trumpet	tous les jours	-	every day

Remember: jouer à   -   for sports and games
              jouer de   -   for musical instruments

le matin - in the morning
l'après-midi - in the afternoon
le soir - evenings, in the evening
le weekend - at the weekend
le mardi - on Tuesdays

Higher

Tu peux expliquer ce que c'est le netball parce que ça n'existe pas en France?
(Can you explain what netball is because it doesn't exist in France).
Oui, c'est un peu comme le basket mais il y a sept personnes dans une équipe et on ne peut pas courir avec le ballon.
(Yes, it's a bit like basketball except there are 7 people in a team and you can't run with the ball).
As-tu jamais joué au netball?
(Have you ever played netball?)
Oui, quand j'étais plus jeune je jouais dans une équipe.
(Yes, when I was younger I played in a team.)

Qu'est-ce que tu penses des boules?
(What do you think of "boules"?)
Je pense que c'est un jeu qui est typiquement français.
(I think it's a game which is typically French.)

Depuis combien de temps est-ce que tu joues au badminton?
(How long have you been playing badminton?)
Depuis cinq ans, j'ai commencé à l'âge de dix ans.
(For 5 years, I started at the age of ten.)

A ton avis, est-ce que c'est une bonne idée de faire du sport?
(In your opinion, is it a good idea to play a sport?)
Je crois que c'est très bon pour la santé de faire de l'exercice.
(I think that it's very good for your health to do some exercise.)

Grammar

Verbs in the Present Tense

The present tense is used to describe what you are doing at the present moment in time, e.g. I am playing tennis, or what you do routinely e.g. I play tennis every day.

French verbs are divided into 3 main groups

- Those that end in -ER e.g. gagner (to win)
- Those that end in -RE e.g. perdre (to lose)
- Those that end in -IR e.g. sortir (to go out) - see p 15.

Each group of verbs has its own basic set of endings which you will need to learn.

Gagner		to win	Perdre		to lose
Je gagne	-	I win/I am winning	Je perds	-	I lose/I am losing
Tu gagnes	-	you win/you are winning	Tu perds	-	you lose/you are losing
Il/elle gagne	-	he/she wins/is winning	Il/elle perd	-	he/she loses/is losing
Nous gagnons	-	we win/we are winning	Nous perdons	-	we lose/we are losing
Vous gagnez	-	you win/you are winning	Vous perdez	-	you lose/you are losing
Ils/elles gagnent	-	they win/they are winning	Ils/elles perdent	-	they lose/they are losing

Make sure that you get the correct ending for the person you are talking about.

eg. 1 - Nous jouons au tennis tous les jours, quelquefois je gagne et quelquefois je perds.
(We play tennis every day, sometimes I win and sometimes I lose.)

eg. 2 - Qu'est-ce que tu fais? - Je joue au tennis. (What are you doing? - I am playing tennis.)

Foundation

Qu'est-ce que tu n'aimes pas faire?
What do you not enjoy doing?
Je déteste regarder le sport à la télé.
(I hate watching sport on TV.)

Qu'est-ce que tu fais le soir/le weekend?
(What do you do in the evening/ at the weekend?)
Le soir, je regarde la télé ou j'écoute de la musique.
Le weekend je fais du sport.
(In the evening I watch TV or listen to music.
At the weekend I so some sport.)

Qu'est-ce que tu aimes faire pendant tes heures libres /à la maison?
(What do you enjoy doing in your free time?/at home?)
J'aime jouer avec l'ordinateur et j'aime lire.
(I like playing on the computer and reading.)

Tu vas souvent au cinéma?
(Do you go to the cinema often?)
Je vais au cinéma une fois par mois.
(I go to the cinema once a month.)

Tu sors souvent avec tes copains?
(Do you go out often with your friends?)
Je sors avec mes copains le weekend.
(I go out with my friends at the weekend.)

Où vas-tu?
(Where do you go?)
Nous allons à la disco ou à une boum.
(We go to the disco or to a party.)

Vocabulary

faire de l'équitation	-	to go horse riding
faire de la natation	-	to go swimming
nager	-	to swim
faire des courses	-	to go shopping
faire du patinage	-	to go ice skating
faire du footing	-	to go jogging
faire du vélo	-	to go cycling
aller chez des copains	-	to go to friends
aller en ville	-	to go to town
aller au cinéma	-	to go to the cinema
un concert	-	a concert
une boum	-	a party
une boîte	-	a night club
une discothèque	-	a disco
sortir	-	to go out
danser	-	to dance
regarder	-	to watch
écouter	-	to listen to
une émission	-	television programme
une comédie	-	a comedy
un feuilleton	-	'soap'
un documentaire	-	documentary
les actualités	-	news

collectionner	-	to collect
lire	-	to read
un roman	-	novel
un roman policier	-	detective novel
un roman d'amour	-	love story
un illustré	-	illustrated magazine
un journal	-	newspaper
un magazine	-	magazine
une revue	-	
la lecture	-	reading
c'est intéressant	-	it is interesting
amusant	-	fun
chouette	-	great
pas mal	-	not bad
ennuyeux	-	boring
bon pour la santé	-	good for your health
à mon avis	-	in my opinion
Je pense que	-	I think that
pas tellement	-	not really
Je ne supporte pas	-	I can't stand
j'ai l'impression que	-	I get the impression that
il me semble que	-	it seems to me that

Higher

Qu'est-ce que tu vas faire le weekend prochain?
(What are you going to do next weekend?)
Je vais jouer au hockey le samedi, j'ai un match l'après-midi et le soir je vais finir mes devoirs parce que nous allons sortir le dimanche.
(I'm going to play hockey on Saturday, I've got a match in the afternoon and in the evening I'm going to finish my homework because we are going to go out on Sunday).

Qu'est-ce que tu as fait la semaine dernière?
(What did you do last week?)
Je suis allée au cinéma avec mon copain, nous avons vu un film de science-fiction. C'était super.
(I went to the cinema with my boyfriend. We saw a science-fiction film. It was excellent).

HOLLYWOOD
MOVIES

Grammar

Regular –ir verbs in the present tense
FINIR

Je finis	-	I finish	Nous finissons	- we finish
Tu finis	-	you finish	Vous finissez	- you finish
Il/elle finit	-	he/she finishes	Ils/elles finissent	- they finish

<u>FAIRE</u> (to do) and <u>ALLER</u> (to go) are two very important but irregular verbs. Both are used frequently when discussing hobbies and interests.

FAIRE

Je fais	-	I do
Tu fais	-	you do
Il/elle fait	-	he/she does
Nous faisons	-	we do
Vous faites	-	you do
Ils/elles font	-	they do

ALLER

Je vais	-	I go
Tu vas	-	you go
Il/elle va	-	he/she goes
Nous allons	-	we go
Vous allez	-	you go
Ils/elles vont	-	they go

In the context of hobbies, faire often means "to go".

 Remember: faire du/de la/de l'/des
Je fais du vélo - I go cycling
Je fais de la natation - I go swimming
Je fais de l'équitation - I go horse riding
Je fais des promenades - I go walking

Remember: aller au/à la/à l'/aux
Je vais au cinéma - I go to the cinema
Je vais à la disco - I go to the disco
Je vais à l'église - I go to church
Je vais aux magasins - I go to the shops

Mini Test

Talk for two minutes in French about your hobbies and interests. Include details such as where? how often? with whom? and your opinion of each hobby. When you are happy with your speech, record it onto tape.

Foundation

Oui, bonne idée, on fait quelque chose après?
(Yes, good idea, shall we do something after?)
On peut aller boire un coup.
(We could go for a drink.)

Est-ce que tu veux sortir ce soir?
(Do you want to go out this evening?)
Je ne peux pas, je suis occupé.
(I can't, I'm busy.)

Où est-ce qu'on se rencontre?
(Where shall we meet?)
Devant le cinéma?
(In front of the cinema?)

Alors tu es libre samedi?
(Are you free on Saturday then?)
Oui, je suis libre le soir.
(Yes I'm free in the evening.)
Ça te dit d'aller au cinéma avec moi?
(Do you fancy going to the cinema with me?)
Oui, qu'est-ce qu'on joue?
(Yes, what's on?)

On se rencontre à quelle heure?
(What time shall we meet?)
A quelle heure commence la séance?
(What time does the showing start?)

A huit heures et demie, on peut se rencontrer à huit heures.
(At 8.30, we could meet at 8pm.)
D'accord.
(OK.)

Il y a un film de science-fiction.
(There is a science fiction film.)
Chouette, j'adore les films de science-fiction.
(Great, I love science fiction films.)

Vocabulary

libre	-	free	un film de guerre	-	war film
occupé(e)	-	busy	un film d'espionnage	-	spy film
sortir	-	to go out	un western	-	a western
se rencontrer	-	to meet	une comédie	-	comedy
se retrouver	-	to meet	un dessin animé	-	cartoon
un rendez-vous	-	a meeting	une pièce de théâtre	-	a play
ensemble	-	together	une séance	-	showing of film
avoir envie de	-	to want to	un concert	-	a concert
ça te dit de (+ infinitive)?	-	do you fancy ?	un spectacle	-	a show
Tu veux?	-	do you want to?	inviter	-	to invite
Tu peux?	-	can you?	une boum	-	a party
D'accord	-	OK	une soirée	-	a get together
Bonne idée	-	good idea	Je regrette	-	I'm sorry
à tout à l'heure	-	see you later	Je ne peux pas	-	I can't
une place	-	seat/ticket (for cinema/theatre)	Je dois	-	I've got to
un billet	-	a ticket	malheureusement	-	unfortunately
un film de science-fiction	-	a science fiction film	Je suis désolé(e)	-	I'm sorry
un film d'horreur	-	a horror film	Zut!	-	damn!
un film d'aventures	-	an adventure film	Quel dommage	-	what a shame
un film d'amour	-	a love story	avec plaisir	-	with pleasure
un film policier	-	detective film			

Higher

D'accord. Moi, je vais réserver les places, et toi tu peux noter ça dans ton agenda.
(Fine. I'll reserve the seats and you can put that in your diary.)

On sort ensemble la semaine prochaine?
(Shall we go out together next week?)
Oui - Tu as envie de voir le nouveau film de James Bond?
(Yes - Would you like to see the new James Bond film?)
Non - J'aimerais mieux aller au théâtre.
Ça te dirait de voir une pièce de Shakespeare?
(No - I would prefer to go to the theatre. Would you like to see a Shakespeare play?)

Bon. Si on se rencontrait à huit heures devant le théâtre vendredi prochain?
(Good. Should we meet at 8 o'clock outside the theatre next Friday?)

Ça te convient d'y aller jeudi soir?
(Does it suit you to go on Thursday evening?)
Non, je suis désolé mais j'ai un rendez-vous jeudi soir.
(No, I'm sorry I've got an appointment on Thursday evening)
Vendredi alors? (Friday then?)
Oui ça me convient mieux (Yes that suits me better)

Grammar

Emphatic Pronouns

In English we can emphasise or stress what we are saying simply by changing our tone of voice; in French an EMPHATIC PRONOUN is required. (Remember that a pronoun is used in place of a noun.)

For je the emphatic pronoun is	moi	For nous the emphatic pronoun is	nous
tu	toi	vous	vous
il	lui	ils	eux
elle	elle	elles	elles
on	soi		

<u>Moi,</u> je vais réserver les places et <u>toi</u> tu peux noter ça dans ton agenda.
<u>I'll</u> reserve the seats and <u>you</u> can put that in your diary.

These pronouns are also used after prepositions:
Tu veux sortir <u>avec moi</u> jeudi? - Désolé(e) mon/ma correspondant(e) arrive demain. Je sors <u>avec lui/elle</u> jeudi.
Do you want to go out <u>with me</u> on Thursday? - I'm sorry, my penfriend arrives tomorrow. I'm going out with <u>him/her</u> on Thursday.

(for other uses of emphatic pronouns, see page 92)

Mini Test

1. Practise inviting someone out; suggest different venues, times and places to meet.

2. Practise accepting and refusing invitations, always giving a good excuse when you refuse!

Foundation

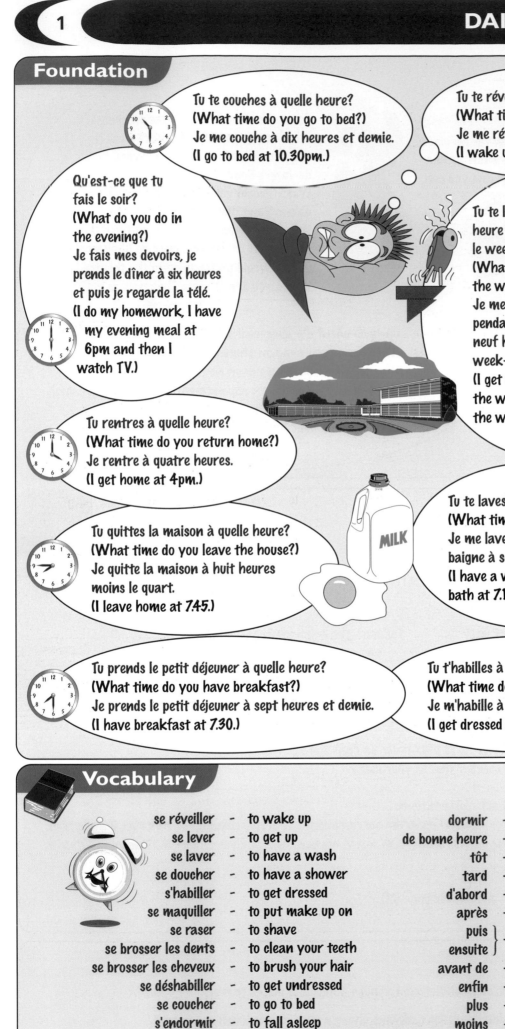

Tu te couches à quelle heure?
(What time do you go to bed?)
Je me couche à dix heures et demie.
(I go to bed at 10.30pm.)

Tu te réveilles à quelle heure?
(What time do you wake up?)
Je me réveille à sept heures.
(I wake up at 7am.)

Qu'est-ce que tu fais le soir?
(What do you do in the evening?)
Je fais mes devoirs, je prends le dîner à six heures et puis je regarde la télé.
(I do my homework, I have my evening meal at 6pm and then I watch TV.)

Tu te lèves à quelle heure pendant la semaine/ le week-end?
(What time do you get up during the week/at the weekend?)
Je me lève à sept heures dix pendant la semaine et à neuf heures et demie le week-end.
(I get up at 10 past 7 during the week and at 9.30 at the weekend.)

Tu rentres à quelle heure?
(What time do you return home?)
Je rentre à quatre heures.
(I get home at 4pm.)

Tu te laves à quelle heure?
(What time do you have a wash?)
Je me lave/Je me douche/Je me baigne à sept heures et quart.
(I have a wash/a shower/a bath at 7.15.)

Tu quittes la maison à quelle heure?
(What time do you leave the house?)
Je quitte la maison à huit heures moins le quart.
(I leave home at 7.45.)

Tu prends le petit déjeuner à quelle heure?
(What time do you have breakfast?)
Je prends le petit déjeuner à sept heures et demie.
(I have breakfast at 7.30.)

Tu t'habilles à quelle heure?
(What time do you get dressed?)
Je m'habille à sept heures vingt-cinq.
(I get dressed at 7.25.)

Vocabulary

se réveiller	-	to wake up	dormir	- to sleep
se lever	-	to get up	de bonne heure	- early
se laver	-	to have a wash	tôt	- early
se doucher	-	to have a shower	tard	- late
s'habiller	-	to get dressed	d'abord	- first of all
se maquiller	-	to put make up on	après	- afterwards
se raser	-	to shave	puis ⎫ ensuite ⎭	- then, next
se brosser les dents	-	to clean your teeth		
se brosser les cheveux	-	to brush your hair	avant de	- before (+ infinitive)
se déshabiller	-	to get undressed	enfin	- finally
se coucher	-	to go to bed	plus	- more
s'endormir	-	to fall asleep	moins	- less

Higher

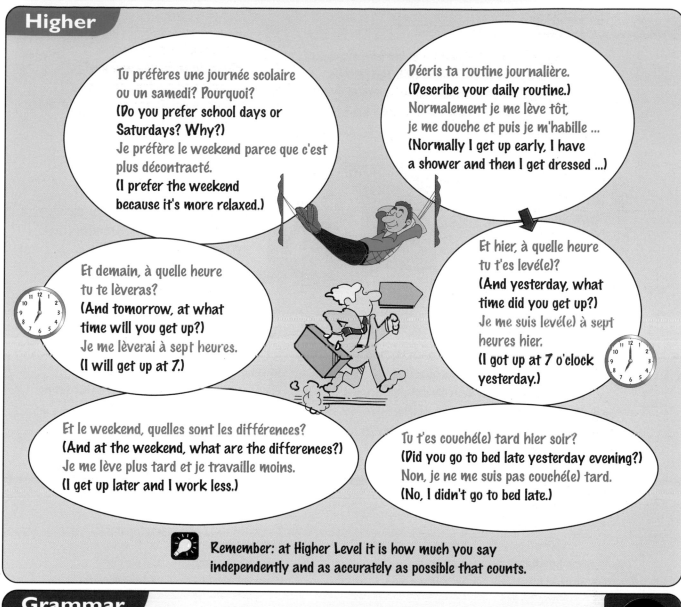

Tu préfères une journée scolaire ou un samedi? Pourquoi?
(Do you prefer school days or Saturdays? Why?)
Je préfère le weekend parce que c'est plus décontracté.
(I prefer the weekend because it's more relaxed.)

Décris ta routine journalière.
(Describe your daily routine.)
Normalement je me lève tôt, je me douche et puis je m'habille ...
(Normally I get up early, I have a shower and then I get dressed ...)

Et demain, à quelle heure tu te lèveras?
(And tomorrow, at what time will you get up?)
Je me lèverai à sept heures.
(I will get up at 7.)

Et hier, à quelle heure tu t'es levé(e)?
(And yesterday, what time did you get up?)
Je me suis levé(e) à sept heures hier.
(I got up at 7 o'clock yesterday.)

Et le weekend, quelles sont les différences?
(And at the weekend, what are the differences?)
Je me lève plus tard et je travaille moins.
(I get up later and I work less.)

Tu t'es couché(e) tard hier soir?
(Did you go to bed late yesterday evening?)
Non, je ne me suis pas couché(e) tard.
(No, I didn't go to bed late.)

Remember: at Higher Level it is how much you say independently and as accurately as possible that counts.

Grammar

The topic "Daily routine" contains a number of common **REFLEXIVE VERBS**: se lever (to get up), se laver (to have a wash), s'habiller (to get dressed), se coucher (to go to bed)). "SE" indicates that the verb is reflexive, i.e. something you do to or for yourself (se laver - to wash oneself, as opposed to laver - to wash something else e.g. laver la voiture - to wash the car). "Se" will change to agree with the subject of the verb as follows:

Se lever (to get (oneself) up)

Je me lève	- I get up	Nous nous levons	-	we get up
Tu te lèves	- you get up	Vous vous levez	-	you get up
Il/elle se lève	- he/she gets up	Ils/Elles se lèvent	-	they get up

Remember - m', t', s' before a vowel as in je m'appelle - I am called.

Note also the position of ne and pas when using a **REFLEXIVE VERB** in the **NEGATIVE**: je <u>ne</u> me lève <u>pas</u> tôt le week-end - I don't get up early at the weekend.

Mini Test

1. Say 10 things about your daily routine, make sure you use at least 5 reflexive verbs and a variety of times.

2. Say 10 different things about your weekend routine.

Foundation

Tu habites une maison ou un appartement?
(Do you live in a house or a flat?)
J'habite une grande maison jumelée.
(I live in a large semi-detached house.)

Tu peux décrire ta maison?
(Can you describe your house?)
C'est moderne et c'est assez grande.
(It's modern and it's quite big.)

Tu peux décrire ta chambre?
(Can you describe your room?)
Oui, elle est très petite, il y a seulement un lit et une armoire. C'est peinte en blanc et rose.
(Yes, it's very small, there is only a bed and a wardrobe. It's decorated in white and pink.)

Il y a combien de pièces?
(How many rooms are there?)
Il y en a huit. Trois au rez-de-chaussée et cinq au premier étage.
(There are 8. 3 downstairs and 5 upstairs.)

Quelles sont ces pièces?
(What rooms are there?)
Il y a le salon, la cuisine, la salle à manger, la salle de bains et 4 chambres.
(There's the lounge, the kitchen, the dining room, the bathroom and 4 bedrooms.)

Est-ce qu'il y a un garage ou un jardin?
(Is there a garage or a garden?)
Oui, les deux. Il y a deux jardins, un devant la maison et un derrière la maison.
(Yes, both. There are 2 gardens, one in front of the house and one behind it.)

Vocabulary

French	English	French	English
une maison	house	une chaîne hi-fi	hi-fi system
une maison individuelle	detached	une platine-laser	CD player
une maison jumelée	semi-detached	un magnétoscope	video recorder
une ferme	farm	un lit	bed
un appartement	flat	des lits superposés (m.)	bunk beds
un bungalow	bungalow	une armoire	wardrobe
une cave	cellar	une commode	chest of drawers
un grenier	loft, attic	une table de chevet	bedside table
un jardin	garden	une étagère	shelf
des arbres	trees (m.)	une chaise	chair
des fleurs	flowers (f.)	un bureau	desk
une pelouse	lawn	une moquette	carpet
une serre	conservatory	des rideaux	curtains
une terrasse	terrace, patio	des posters	posters
un hall d'entrée / un vestibule	hall	au mur	on the wall
un salon	living room	par terre	on the floor
une salle à manger	dining room	à gauche de	on the left
une cuisine	kitchen	à droite de	on the right
une buanderie	utility room	au milieu de	in the middle of
une chambre	bedroom	au-dessus de	above
une salle de bains	bathroom	au-dessous de	underneath
un WC	toilet	bien rangé(e)	tidy
une douche	shower	en désordre	untidy
une pièce	room	partager	to share
une télévision	television		

Remember: du/de la/de l'/des

Higher

Décris ta maison idéale.
(Describe your ideal home.)
Ma maison idéale serait*
énorme avec vingt pièces,
une piscine et un terrain
de tennis.
(My ideal home would be
enormous, with 20 rooms,
a swimming pool and
a tennis court.)

Tu habites ta maison depuis combien de temps?
(How long have you been living in your house?)
J'y habite depuis quatre ans.
(I have been living there 4 years.)

Ta chambre te plaît?
(Do you like your bedroom?)
Ma chambre me plaît assez; j'aime
les meubles mais je n'aime pas la
couleur des murs.
(I quite like my bedroom; I like
the furniture but I don't like
the colour of the walls.)

* for notes on the formation
and use of the conditional,
see page 37.

Comment changerais-tu ta chambre?
(How would you change your bedroom?)
Je changerais* les rideaux et le tapis.
(I would change the curtains and the rug.)

Grammar

Question Words

Quand?	- when?	Comment?	- how?
Qui?	- who?	Combien?	- how many/how much?
Qu'est-ce que?	- what?	Où?	- where?
Quel/quelle/quels/quelles?	- which?	Pourquoi?	- why?

Remember: Est-ce que? - is it that? (see explanation)

It is important that you understand exactly what you are being asked in an exam situation, therefore it is essential that you memorise these question words. Examiners are also impressed if you can form questions yourself, so here are some tips:

1. Using "est-ce que" (literal translation - "is it that...") in front of a statement is a very common French way of forming a question, especially when speaking.

   eg. Tu habites une maison. (You live in a house.)
   Est-ce que tu habites une maison? (Do you live in a house?)
   Tu habites avec ta mère. (You live with your mother.)
   Est-ce que tu habites avec ta mère? (Do you live with your mother?)

2. Use a question word.
   eg. Où habites-tu? (notice the word order has changed - verb and then subject.) (Where do you live?)
   Qui habite avec toi? (Who lives with you?)

3. You can use intonation to make a statement sound like a question - just make your voice go up at the end.
   eg. Tu as ta propre chambre. (You have your own room.)
   Tu as ta propre chambre? (Have you got your own room?)

4. Sometimes you can invert the subject and verb to change a statement into a question.
   eg. Tu partages ta chambre. (You share your bedroom.)
   Partages-tu ta chambre? (Do you share your bedroom?)

Foundation

Comment dépenses-tu ton argent?
(What do you spend your money on?)
J'achète des vêtements et des CDs.
(I buy clothes and CDs.)

Tu reçois de l'argent de poche?
(Do you get pocket money?)
Combien?
(How much?)
Je reçois cinq livres par semaine de mes parents.
(I get £5 a week from my parents.)

Tu gagnes combien? Quelles sont tes heures de travail?
(How much do you earn? How many hours do you work?)
Je gagne vingt livres par jour; je travaille le samedi de neuf heures à cinq heures.
(I earn £20 a day; I work Saturdays from 9am to 5pm.)

Est-ce que tu dois aider à la maison?
(Do you have to help with the housework?)
Oui, je dois ranger ma chambre et promener le chien.
(Yes, I have to tidy my room and walk the dog.)

Que fais-tu pour gagner de l'argent? Tu as un petit travail/boulot?
(What do you do to earn money? Do you have a part-time job?)
Je fais du baby-sitting de temps en temps et le samedi je travaille chez une coiffeuse.
(I babysit from time to time and on Saturdays I work in a hairdresser's.)

Vocabulary

French		English	French		English
faire le ménage	-	to do the housework	repasser	-	to iron
faire la vaisselle	-	to do the washing up	l'argent de poche	-	pocket money
faire la lessive	-	to do the washing	donner	-	to give
faire la cuisine	-	to do the cooking	gagner	-	to earn
faire les courses	-	to do the shopping	recevoir	-	to receive
faire du jardinage	-	to do the gardening	dépenser	-	to spend
faire du bricolage	-	to do some DIY	acheter	-	to buy
faire mon lit	-	to make my bed	faire des économies	-	to save
faire du baby-sitting	-	to babysit	une livre	-	a pound sterling
passer l'aspirateur	-	to hoover	par mois	-	per month
ranger ma chambre	-	to tidy my bedroom	par semaine	-	per week
laver la voiture	-	to clean the car	travailler	-	to work
promener le chien	-	to walk the dog	chez une coiffeuse	-	at a hairdresser's
mettre la table	-	to set the table	dans un magasin	-	in a shop
débarrasser la table	-	to clear the table	comme caissier/caissière	-	as a cashier
sortir la poubelle	-	to put the rubbish out	livrer les journaux	-	to deliver newspapers
vider le lave-vaisselle	-	to empty the dishwasher			

HOUSEHOLD CHORES, POCKET MONEY

Higher

Qu'est-ce que tu as fait pour aider à la maison hier?
(What did you do to help at home yesterday?)

Et la semaine prochaine, qu'est-ce que tu en feras?
(And next week, what will you do with it?)
Je ferai encore des économies et peut-être que j'achèterai quelque chose.
(I'll save some more and maybe I'll buy something.)

J'ai rangé ma chambre comme d'habitude et j'ai fait la cuisine.
(I tidied my room as usual and I cooked.)

Qu'est-ce tu as fait avec ton argent de poche la semaine dernière?
(What did you do with your pocket money last week?)
J'ai mis 10 livres à la banque comme toujours et j'ai acheté un nouveau pantalon.
(I put £10 in the bank as always and I bought a new pair of trousers.)

Est-ce que tu en fais plus que ton frère/père?
(Do you do more than your brother/father?)
Je fais des choses différentes - par exemple mon frère ne fait jamais le repassage.
(I do different things - for example, my brother never does the ironing.)

Grammar

The Negative

To make a sentence negative in French (ie. saying something is <u>not</u>, <u>never</u>, <u>no longer</u>, etc.) you need two words:

ne ... pas	-	not	ne ... rien	-	nothing
ne ... plus	-	no more, no longer	ne ... personne	-	nobody
ne ... jamais	-	never	NB: ne ... que	-	only

These two words go around the main verb in the sentence as follows:

a. Je <u>ne</u> fais <u>pas</u> le ménage - I <u>don't</u> do the housework.
   Je <u>n'</u>aime <u>pas</u> travailler dans le jardin - I <u>don't</u> like gardening.

b. Nous avons maintenant un lave-vaisselle, alors je <u>ne</u> fais <u>plus</u> la vaisselle - Now that we have a dishwasher, I <u>no longer</u> wash up.

c. Je lave la voiture, mais je <u>ne</u> reçois <u>rien</u> - I wash the car, but I receive nothing for it.

d. Je <u>ne</u> range <u>jamais</u> ma chambre - I <u>never</u> tidy my room.

e. Je <u>ne</u> vois <u>personne</u> travailler dans le jardin - I <u>can't</u> see <u>anyone</u> working in the garden.

f. NB! Je ne fais pas beaucoup à la maison, je <u>ne</u> fais <u>que</u> mon lit - I don't do much to help at home, I <u>only</u> make my bed.

For other negative expressions, see Grammar Summary page 90.

Mini Test

1. Describe what the person responsible for most of the household chores in your house does in a typical day.

2. Make a list in French of what you have spent your money on over the last month.

3. Explain how/from where you get/earn your money.

Foundation

Tu peux décrire une journée typique au collège?
(Can you describe a typical day at school?)
Je commence à neuf heures, il y a une récréation à onze heures, le déjeuner est à une heure et puis je finis à trois heures et demie.
(I start at 9 o'clock, there's a break at 11 o'clock, lunch is at one o'clock and then I finish at 3.30.)

Il est comment ton collège?
(What is your school like?)
Mon collège est grand et moderne.
(My school is big and modern.)

Il y a combien d'élèves et de professeurs?
(How many pupils and teachers are there?)
Il y a huit cents élèves et quarante profs.
(There are 800 pupils and 40 teachers.)

Qu'est-ce que tu n'aimes pas?
(What don't you like?)
Je n'aime pas la technologie - c'est trop difficile.
(I don't like Technology - it's too difficult)

Il y a combien de cours par jour?
(How many lessons are there a day?)
Il y en a sept.
(There are seven.)

Quelle est ta matière préférée?
(What is your favourite subject?)
Je préfère les maths parce que c'est utile.
(I prefer maths because it's useful.)

Les cours commencent à quelle heure?
(What time do lessons start?)
Ils commencent à neuf heures. (They start at 9 O'clock.)
Ils finissent à quelle heure? (What time do they finish?)
Ils finissent à trois heures et demie. (They finish at 3.30.)

Tu as beaucoup de devoirs?
(Do you have a lot of homework?)
J'en ai trois heures tous les soirs.
(I have 3 hours every evening.)

Qu'est-ce que tu étudies?
(What do you study?)
J'étudie l'anglais, le français, les maths et 6 autres matières.
(I study English, French, maths and 6 other subjects.)

Vocabulary

l'école	-	school (general)	ennuyeux(euse)	-	boring
le collège	-	school (age 11-16)	amusant(e)	-	fun
le lycée	-	school (age 16-18)	utile	-	useful
la matière	-	subject	inutile	-	useless
le cours	-	lesson	l'histoire	-	history
étudier	-	to study	la géographie	-	geography
apprendre	-	to learn	les mathématiques	-	maths
enseigner	-	to teach	l'anglais	-	English
le professeur	-	teacher	le français	-	French
la récréation	-	break	l'espagnol	-	Spanish
le déjeuner	-	lunch	l'allemand	-	German
l'emploi du temps	-	timetable	les sciences	-	sciences
les devoirs	-	homework	la physique	-	physics
la salle de classe	-	classroom	la chimie	-	chemistry
l'uniforme scolaire	-	school uniform	la biologie	-	biology
facile	-	easy	la technologie	-	technology
difficile	-	difficult	l'informatique	-	I.T.
intéressant(e)	-	interesting	le dessin	-	art
important(e)	-	important	la musique	-	music
pratique	-	practical	l'éducation physique	-	P.E.

Higher

Ton collège a une bonne réputation?
(Does your school have a good reputation?)
Oui, nous avons de bons résultats, et les profs sont gentils et travailleurs.
(Yes, we get good results and the teachers are kind and hardworking.)

Qu'est-ce que tu as étudié hier?
(What did you have yesterday?)
Hier j'ai eu deux heures de technologie et une heure de français avant le déjeuner et deux heures de musique après le déjeuner.)
(Yesterday I had 2 hours of technology and one hour of French before lunch and two hours of music after lunch.)

Tu crois que l'uniforme scolaire est une bonne idée?
(Do you think that school uniform is a good idea?)
Oui, c'est très pratique, on sait ce qu'il faut porter et notre uniforme me plaît.
(Yes, it's very practical, you know what to wear and I like our uniform.)

À ton avis quelle est la matière la plus intéressante, la musique ou la technologie?
(In your opinion which is the most interesting, music or technology?)
La technologie est plus intéressante que la musique parce que c'est utile mais la matière la plus utile pour moi c'est l'anglais.
(Technology is more interesting than music because it's useful but the most useful subject for me is English.)

Tu es fort(e) en langues?
(Are you good at languages?)
Oui je suis assez fort(e) en français.
Je comprends bien et j'adore écouter la langue.
(Yes I am quite good at French. I understand well and I love listening to the language.)

Grammar   Comparative and superlative of adjectives

If you want to compare two things or say which you think is the best, here's what you need to do:

use either   plus intéressant que   (more interesting than)
             moins intéressant que   (less interesting than)
         or aussi intéressant que   (as interesting as)

e.g. Le français est plus intéressant que l'anglais (French is more interesting than English)

You may need to make your adjectives agree:

e.g. La musique est plus importante que le dessin (Music is more important than art)

or   Les sciences sont aussi importantes que les maths (Sciences are as important as maths)

To say which you think is the best, worst, most interesting, etc, you need to put le, la or les in front.

e.g. La matière la plus importante c'est l'informatique (The most important subject is IT)
      Le cours le plus ennuyeux c'est l'histoire (The most boring lesson is history)
      Les devoirs les plus difficiles sont les devoirs de maths (The most difficult homework is maths)

Again adjectives need to agree if necessary.

As always, one or two adjectives are irregular:

e.g. bon   meilleur   le meilleur   mauvais   pire   le pire
      (good)   (better)   (the best)   (bad)   (worse)   (the worst)

Il est le meilleur prof du monde.   L'anglais est pire que l'histoire.
(He's the best teacher in the world.)   (English is worse than history.)

Foundation

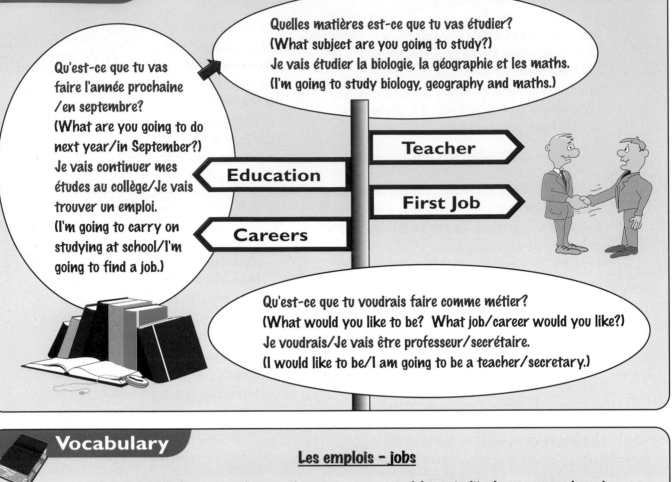

Qu'est-ce que tu vas faire l'année prochaine /en septembre?
(What are you going to do next year/in September?)
Je vais continuer mes études au collège/Je vais trouver un emploi.
(I'm going to carry on studying at school/I'm going to find a job.)

Quelles matières est-ce que tu vas étudier?
(What subject are you going to study?)
Je vais étudier la biologie, la géographie et les maths.
(I'm going to study biology, geography and maths.)

Education

Careers

Teacher

First Job

Qu'est-ce que tu voudrais faire comme métier?
(What would you like to be? What job/career would you like?)
Je voudrais/Je vais être professeur/secrétaire.
(I would like to be/I am going to be a teacher/secretary.)

Vocabulary

Les emplois – jobs

un agent de police	- policeman/woman	un(e) ouvrier(ière)	- manual worker
un(e) avocat(e)	- lawyer	un plombier	- plumber
un(e) boucher(ère)	- butcher	un pompier	- firefighter
un(e) boulanger(ère)	- baker	un(e) professeur	- teacher
un chef de cuisine	- chef	un(e) programmeur(euse)	- computer programmer
un(e) coiffeur(euse)	- hairdresser	un(e) secrétaire	- secretary
un(e) comptable	- accountant	un(e) technicien(ienne)	- technician
un(e) dentiste	- dentist	un(e) vendeur(euse)	- sales person
un(e) électricien(ienne)	- electrician	un vétérinaire	- vet
un(e) employé(e) de banque	- bank clerk	travailler dans	- to work in
un(e) employé(e) de bureau	- office worker	une banque	- a bank
un(e) facteur/trice	- postman/woman	un bureau	- an office
un homme/une femme d'affaires	- businessman/woman	un hôpital	- a hospital
un(e) infirmier(ière)	- nurse	une usine	- a factory
un(e) journaliste	- journaliste	travailler avec	- to work with
un maçon	- builder	les enfants	- children
un(e) mécanicien(ienne)	- mechanic	les machines	- machines
un médecin	- doctor	les animaux	- animals

Remember: Je voudrais être journaliste - I would like to be a journalist
Je vais devenir vétérinaire - I am going to be a vet

Do not use with un/une when talking about your own future career or someone else's career:

Mon frère est comptable - my brother is an accountant

Higher

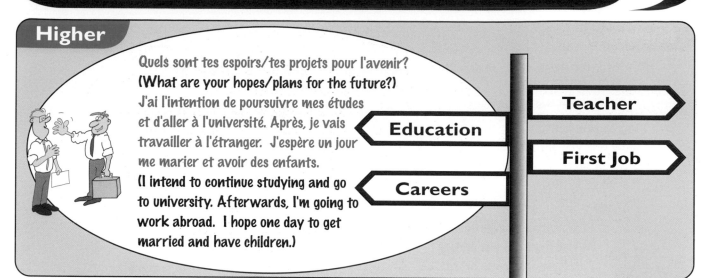

Quels sont tes espoirs/tes projets pour l'avenir?
(What are your hopes/plans for the future?)
J'ai l'intention de poursuivre mes études
et d'aller à l'université. Après, je vais
travailler à l'étranger. J'espère un jour
me marier et avoir des enfants.
(I intend to continue studying and go
to university. Afterwards, I'm going to
work abroad. I hope one day to get
married and have children.)

Education

Careers

Teacher

First Job

Grammar

The Future Tense I

Just as in English, ALLER + INFINITIVE can be used to express what is going to happen.

Je vais quitter le collège - I'm going to leave school
Il va trouver un emploi - He is going to find a job
Elle va faire un apprentissage - She is going to do an apprenticeship

The verb ALLER is written in full on page 15.

The Future Tense II

The future tense in French is formed by adding a modified version of the verb AVOIR to the INFINITIVE.
The future tense endings are as follows:

Je travaillerai	- I shall work
Tu travailleras	- you will work
Il/elle travaillera	- he/she will work
nous travaillerons	- we will work
vous travaillerez	- you will work
Ils/elles travailleront	- they will work

Je finirai mes études - I shall finish my studies

Regular -re verbs drop the final "e" of the
infinitive before adding the future tense endings:

Je poursuivrai mes études - I shall continue studying
(poursuivre - to continue, pursue)

Expressions of future time:

ce soir	- this evening
demain	- tomorrow
après-demain	- the day after tomorrow
la semaine prochaine	- next week
l'année prochaine	- next year
dans cinq ans	- in 5 years
à l'avenir	- in the future

> Verbs which are IRREGULAR
> in the future tense can be
> found on the next page.

Mini Test

1. Prepare a speech in French about your school. Mention the subjects you do, your opinion of them and describe one of your teachers.

2. Record yourself on tape talking about your future plans. What are your plans for:
   next September (en septembre)
   in 2 years time (dans 2 ans)
   in 10 years time (dans 10 ans)

Higher

D'abord, qu'est-ce que tu devras faire, avant de te présenter pour un entretien?
(First of all, what will you have to do before you arrive for an interview?)

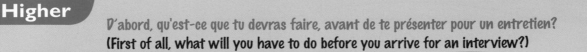

Tu iras comment?
(How will you get there?)
J'irai en taxi.
(I shall go by taxi.)

Qu'est-ce que tu feras pour te préparer?
(What will you do to prepare yourself?)
Je préparerai les réponses aux questions possibles.
(I shall prepare answers to possible questions.)

Tu arriveras à quelle heure?
(What time will you arrive?)
J'arriverai de bonne heure.
(I shall arrive early.)

Qu'est-ce que tu porteras?
(What will you wear?)
Je porterai un costume/un ensemble.
(I shall wear a suit (male/female).)

Grammar

Irregular Verbs in The Future Tense

Some very common verbs are irregular in the future tense. The first part of the verb (the stem) changes, but the endings remain the same. Some common irregular future stems are:

aller to go	–	j'irai I shall go	pouvoir to be able to	–	je pourrai I shall be able to

aller
to go – j'irai
I shall go

avoir
to have – j'aurai
I shall have

devoir
to have to – je devrai
I shall have to

envoyer
to send – j'enverrai
I shall send

être
to be – je serai
I shall be

faire
to do – je ferai
I shall do

pleuvoir
to rain – il pleuvra
it will rain

pouvoir
to be able to – je pourrai
I shall be able to

recevoir
to receive – je recevrai
I shall receive

savoir
to know (facts) – je saurai
I shall know

venir
to come – je viendrai
I shall come

voir
to see – je verrai
I shall see

vouloir
to want to – je voudrai
I shall want to

With some verbs there is just a slight change to the stem:

acheter
to buy – j'achèterai
I shall buy

appeler
to call – j'appellerai
I shall call

jeter
to throw – je jetterai
I shall throw

lever
to lift/raise – je lèverai
I shall lift/raise

nettoyer
to clean – je nettoierai
I shall clean

NB: Note the use of the future tense after quand (when) where we would use the present tense in English:

Quand j'aurai dix-huit ans, j'irai à l'université
(When I am (shall be, in French) 18, I shall go to university.)

Quand je quitterai l'université, j'achèterai une voiture.
(When I (shall) leave university, I shall buy a car.

Higher

You may be expected to answer questions in French in an interview situation. At Foundation Level, this will involve talking about your personal details and qualities (pages 8 and 9), your interests (pages 12 to 15), and possibly your education (pages 24 and 25). At Higher Level the questions will be more demanding, and will require use of different tenses:

Pourquoi est-ce que vous voulez cet emploi?
(Why do you want this job?)
J'ai toujours voulu travailler dans un bureau et j'ai les qualités et l'expérience nécessaires.
(I've always wanted to work in an office and I've got the necessary qualities and experience.)

Qu'est-ce que vous avez étudié au collège?
(What subjects have you studied at school?)
J'ai étudié les maths, l'anglais, le français, etc.
(I have studied maths, English, French, etc.)

Est-ce que vous avez de l'expérience pour cet emploi?
(Do you have any experience for this job?)
Oui, je travaille dans un magasin le samedi depuis deux ans.
(Yes, I have been working in a shop on Saturdays for 2 years.)
Oui, j'ai fait un stage dans un bureau il y a quelques mois.
(Yes, I did my work experience in an office a few months ago.)

Parlez-moi un peu de votre expérience professionnelle.
(Tell me about your professional experience.)
J'ai travaillé dans un bureau pendant deux semaines. J'ai parlé le français au téléphone et j'ai fait du traitement de texte.
(I worked in an office for 2 weeks. I spoke French on the telephone and I did some word-processing.)

NB: As this a formal interview situation, the "vous" form of address is used.

Grammar

The Perfect Tense with Avoir

The PERFECT TENSE is one of the past tenses in French (talking about something that has happened and is completed and over and done with). It is made up of two parts: an AUXILIARY (helping) verb, either Avoir or Etre and a PAST PARTICIPLE. We will look here at verbs which take Avoir (Remind yourself of the verb avoir - see page 9.)

The PAST PARTICIPLE of regular verbs is formed in the following way:

-ER verbs: travailler (to work) becomes travaillé
-IR verbs: finir (to finish) becomes fini
-RE verbs: vendre (to sell) becomes vendu

J'ai travaillé de neuf heures à cinq heures. (I worked from 9am to 5pm.)

Il a fini son stage la semaine dernière. (He finished his work experience last week.)

Nous avons répondu aux questions des clients. (We answered the customers' questions.)

As with the future tense, there are a number of very common verbs which have IRREGULAR PAST PARTICIPLES, which must be learnt. Here are some examples of irregular past participles of verbs which take AVOIR:

devoir (to have to do something) - j'ai dû - I (have) had to, did have to
écrire (to write) - j'ai écrit - I wrote, have written, did write
faire (to do) - j'ai fait - I did, have done, did do
prendre (to take) - j'ai pris - I took, have taken, did take

See grammar summary page 88 for an extensive list of irregular past participles.

Foundation

Qu'est-ce qu'il y a pour les touristes?
(What is there for tourists?)
Le centre commercial est très connu, aussi
on peut visiter Oxford ou Cambridge en autobus.
(The shopping centre is very well-known,
also you can visit Oxford or Cambridge by bus.)

Tu habites une ville ou un village?
(Do you live in a town or a village?)
J'habite en centre ville/J'habite
un petit village.
(I live in the town centre/I live
in a little village.)

Qu'est-ce qu'on peut faire le soir?
(What can you do in the evening?)
On peut aller en boîte, on peut manger
au restaurant ou on peut aller au pub.
(You can go to a club, you can eat in a
restaurant or you can go to a pub.)

Où se trouve Milton Keynes?
(Where is Milton Keynes?)
Milton Keynes se trouve dans le sud-est de
l'Angleterre, à quatre-vingts kilomètres de Londres.
(Milton Keynes is in the South East of
England, 80 km from London.)

Qu'est-ce qu'on peut faire
à Milton Keynes pendant la journée?
(What can you do in Milton Keynes
during the day?)
On peut faire des courses, on peut aller
à la patinoire et on peut jouer aux boules.
(You can go shopping, you can
go to the skating rink and
you can go bowling.)

Qu'est-ce qu'il y a à Milton Keynes?
(What is there in Milton Keynes?)
Il y a un cinéma, un théâtre et
beaucoup de magasins.
(There is a cinema, a theatre
and lots of shops.)

Vocabulary

une ville	-	a town	un château	-	a castle
un village	-	a village	un hôtel de ville	-	a town hall
en centre ville	-	in the town centre	un bar	-	a bar
à la campagne	-	in the countryside	un restaurant	-	a restaurant
dans les banlieues	-	in the suburbs	un musée	-	a museum
les environs	-	the outskirts	un magasin	-	a shop
se trouver	-	to be situated	un supermarché	-	a supermarket
près de	-	near to	un centre sportif	-	a sports centre
loin de	-	far from	un bureau de poste	-	a post office
la région	-	the area	un marché	-	a market
le coin	-	the area	une église	-	a church
			une cathédrale	-	a cathedral
on peut	-	you can	une gare	-	a station
visiter	-	to visit	une banque	-	a bank
			une bibliothèque	-	a library
sale	-	dirty			
propre	-	clean	le nord	-	north
pollué(e)	-	polluted	l'est	-	east
bruyant(e)	-	noisy	le sud	-	south
barbant(e)	-	boring	l'ouest	-	west
tranquille	-	peaceful	le nord-est	-	the north east
isolé(e)	-	isolated	le centre	-	centre

Higher

Préférerais*-tu habiter à la campagne ou en ville? Pourquoi?
(Would you prefer to live in the countryside or in a town? Why?)
Je préférerais* habiter à la campagne parce que c'est très tranquille.
(I would prefer to live in the countryside because it's very peaceful.)
Je préférerais* habiter en ville parce qu'il y a toujours beaucoup de choses à faire.
(I would prefer to live in town because there are always plenty of things to do.)

Quels sont les avantages et les inconvénients d'habiter en ville/à la campagne?
(What are the advantages and disadvantages of living in town/in the countryside?)
En ville, il y a beaucoup de magasins et d'autobus. On peut aller au cinéma et au théâtre, mais d'un côté, il y a trop de bruit et de circulation.
(In town, there are lots of shops and buses. You can go to the cinema and theatre, but on the other hand, there is too much noise and traffic.)

A la campagne, l'air est propre, c'est très pittoresque et on peut faire des randonnées à pied. Mais souvent il n'y a rien à faire et il y a peu d'autobus.
(In the countryside the air is clean, it's very picturesque and one can go walking. But often there is nothing to do and there are few buses.)

*For notes on the conditional "I would ...", see page 37.

Grammar

We have used the phrase "on peut ... " (one can) several times in this section.
POUVOIR (to be able to) is one of the modal verbs i.e. a verb mainly used with an infinitive, e.g. on peut faire toutes sortes de sports - you can do all kinds of sports.

POUVOIR - to be able to

Je peux	-	I can
Tu peux	-	you can
il/elle peut	-	he/she can
nous pouvons	-	we can
vous pouvez	-	you can
ils/elles peuvent	-	they can

Pouvoir + infinitive
Il y a un lac. Je peux y faire de la planche à voile.
(There is a lake. I can go windsurfing there.)
Nous pouvons aller souvent en boîte de nuit.
(We can often go to a night club.)

Mini Test

1. How many buildings can you name in French in one minute? Stop, and check vocabulary on the opposite page.

2. Describe your town/village in French, listing the facilities available, and what one can do there. Record yourself on tape.

3. Draw up 2 lists in French: one of advantages of living in your town/village, and one of disadvantages. Try to make them of equal length!

Foundation

Quel temps faisait-il?
(What was the weather like?)
Il faisait chaud.
(It was hot.)

Où est-ce que tu prends tes vacances normalement?
(Where do you normally spend your holidays?)
D'habitude, nous allons au bord de la mer.
(We usually go to the seaside.)

Tu pars pour combien de temps et avec qui?
(How long do you go for, and who do you go with?)
Nous partons normalement pour deux semaines en famille.
(We normally go for 2 weeks together as a family.)

Où as-tu logé?
(Where did you stay?)
Nous sommes resté(e)s dans un hôtel.
(We stayed in a hotel.)

Qu'est-ce que tu as fait pendant les vacances?
(What did you do during the holidays?)
Pendant la journée, on est allé à la plage, et le soir nous sommes allé(e)s dans les bars.
(During the day, we went to the beach, and in the evening, we went to bars.)

Où as-tu passé les grandes vacances l'année dernière?
(Where did you spend your holiday last summer?)
Je suis allé(e) en Grèce avec des copains pour trois semaines.
(I went to Greece with friends for 3 weeks.)

Tu y es allé(e) comment?
(How did you travel?)
Nous sommes allé(e)s en avion.
(We went by plane.)

Vocabulary

les vacances	- holidays	il fait/il faisait	- it is/it was
les grandes vacances	- summer holidays	beau	- fine
les vacances de Noël	- Chrismas holidays	chaud	- hot
de Pâques	- Easter holidays	du soleil	- sunny
en France	- to, in France	du vent	- windy
en Angleterre	- to, in England	froid	- cold
en Espagne	- to, in Spain	mauvais	- bad weather
en Italie	- to, in Italy	il pleut/il pleuvait	- it is/was rainy
en Grèce	- to, in Greece	il gèle/gelait	- it is/was freezing
à Londres	- to, in London	il neige/neigeait	- it is/was snowing
à Paris	- to, in Paris	il est/il était...	- it is/was...
à l'étranger	- abroad	couvert/nuageux	- overcast/cloudy
à la maison	- at home	il y a/il y avait de l'orage	- there is/was a storm
au bord de la mer	- by the sea	la météo	- weather report
à la campagne	- in the country	confortable	- comfortable
à la montagne	- in the mountains	de grand confort	- very comfortable
à la plage	- to, on the beach	de grand luxe	- luxurious
se bronzer	- to sunbathe, get a tan	pas (trop) cher	- not (too) expensive
se baigner	- to swim, bathe		
visiter la région	- to visit the area		
visiter les environs	- to visit the surrounding area		
le temps	- the weather		

Higher

Parle-moi un peu de tes vacances l'été dernier.
(Tell me about your holiday last summer.)
Je suis allé(e) en Allemagne en famille. On est parti en voiture et on est descendu chez des amis pour quelques jours. Puis on est reparti pour le sud de l'Allemagne où on a fait du camping. Il faisait un temps splendide.
(I went to Germany with my family. We went by car and stayed with friends for a few days. Then we set off again for South Germany where we camped. The weather was marvellous.)

Quels sont tes projets pour les grandes vacances?
(What are your plans for the summer holidays?)
J'irai passer une quinzaine chez mon/ma correspondant(e) à Paris. On visitera des monuments historiques et on fera du lèche-vitrine.
(I'm going to spend a fortnight with my penfriend in Paris. We will visit some historic monuments and do some window shopping.)

Où est-ce que tu aimerais passer tes vacances si tu étais libre de choisir?
Where would you like to spend your holidays if you had a free choice?
J'aimerais aller aux Etats-Unis pour voir le Grand Canyon.
I would like to visit the United States and see the Grand Canyon.

Grammar

The Perfect Tense with Être

We have already met those verbs which take AVOIR in the perfect tense. A few very common verbs form the perfect tense with ÊTRE as the auxiliary verb. The past participle of these verbs agrees with the subject in the same way that adjectives agree with nouns.

e.g. Marie est arriv<u>ée</u>.   Marie (has) arrived, did arrive.
  Les garçons sont arriv<u>és</u>. The boys (have) arrived, did arrive.

ALLER - to go

Je suis allé(e)	-	I went, did go	nous sommes allé(e)s - we went
Tu es allé(e)	-	you went, did go	vous êtes allé(e)(s) - you went
il est allé	-	he went	ils sont allés - they went
elle est allée	-	she went	elles sont allées - they went

Some other verbs which form the perfect tense with être are:

				Past Participle					Past Participle
venir	-	to come	-	venu	monter	-	to go up	-	monté
arriver	-	to arrive	-	arrivé	descendre	-	to go down	-	descendu
partir	-	to leave	-	parti	rester	-	to remain	-	resté
sortir	-	to go out	-	sorti	retourner	-	to return	-	retourné

For a complete list of verbs with être in the perfect tense, see Grammar Summary page 87.

Mini Test

Record yourself on tape talking about a holiday in the past, and plans for your next holiday. Pay very careful attention to tenses and include as much detail as possible.

Foundation

Le Voyage/The Journey
Salut Daniel, je te présente ma mère.
(Hello Daniel, let me introduce you to my mother.)
Bonjour Madame, enchanté
(Hello, pleased to meet you.)
Tu as fait bon voyage?
(Have you had a good journey?)
Oui, merci, un peu fatigant, mais ça va.
(Yes, thanks, a bit tiring but OK.)

Le soir/Le matin - In the evening/morning
Bonne nuit, dors bien.
(Goodnight, sleep well.)
Bonjour, tu as bien dormi?
(Good morning, did you sleep well?)

A la maison/At the house
Tu as faim? Tu as soif?
(Are you hungry? Are you thirsty?)
Non, ça va, mais je suis très fatigué.
(No, I'am OK, but I'm very tired.)
Alors, je te montre ta chambre.
(I'll show you your bedroom then.)

A table/At table
Tu veux encore des haricots?
(Do you want some more beans?)
Oui, je veux bien.
(Yes, I'd love some.)
Sers-toi.
(Help yourself.)
Tu peux me passer le pain?
(Can you pass me the bread?)

Où est la salle de bains, s'il vous plaît?
(Where is the bathroom, please?)
C'est juste à côté de ta chambre.
Tu as une serviette?
(It's just next to your bedroom.
Have you got a towel?)
Oui, j'en ai une merci.
(Yes, I've got one thanks.)

Des problèmes/Problems
J'ai oublié mon sèche-cheveux.
(I've forgotten my hairdryer.)
Tu peux emprunter le mien.
(You can borrow mine.)

Remember: use "tu" when talking to your penfriend, but "vous" to his parents unless they tell you otherwise.

Vocabulary

tutoyer	-	to call someone "tu"	un sèche-cheveux	- hairdryer
enchanté(e) de faire } votre connaissance	-	pleased to meet you	du savon	- soap
			prêter	- to lend
se présenter	-	to introduce yourself	emprunter	- to borrow
avoir faim	-	to be hungry	sers-toi	- help yourself
avoir soif	-	to be thirsty	fais comme chez toi	- make yourself at home
avoir sommeil	-	to be sleepy	Je ne sais pas	- I don't know
fatigué(e)	-	tired	Je ne comprends pas	- I don't understand
fatigant	-	tiring	comment dit-on ...?	- How do you say ...?
ça va (?)	-	I'm fine/How are you?	Pardon	- excuse me/sorry
comme ci, comme ça	-	so so	Excusez-moi	- excuse me
montrer	-	to show	Je suis désolé(e)	- I'm sorry
une serviette	-	towel	bienvenu(e)	- welcome

Higher

Bienvenu/Welcome

Maman, voici mon correspondant anglais, il s'appelle James.
(Mum, here's my English penfriend, his name is James)
Bonjour James, bienvenu en France. Fais comme chez toi.
(Hello James, welcome to France. Make yourself at home.)
Merci Madame, est-ce que je peux téléphoner à mes parents?
(Thank you, may I phone my parents?)

Au revoir/Goodbye

Je vous remercie, Madame, pour votre hospitalité. J'espère revenir un jour.
(Thank you for your hospitality. I hope to come back one day.)
Il n'y a pas de quoi, tu es toujours le bienvenu chez nous.
(It was a pleasure, you're always welcome here.)

La nourriture/Food

Tu aimes la cuisine française, James?
(Do you like French cooking, James?)
Oui, je l'adore, surtout le pain.
(Yes, I love it, especially the bread.)
Est-ce qu'il y a quelque chose que tu n'aimes pas?
(Is there anything you don't like?)
Seulement les fruits de mer, je les déteste.
(Only seafood, I hate it.)

Sortir/Going out

Qu'est-ce qu'on fait aujourd'hui, James?
(What shall we do today, James?)
ça m'est égal. (I don't mind.)
Si on allait à la piscine, tu aimes la natation?
(How about going to the swimming pool. Do you like swimming?)
Oui, bonne idée, j'adore ça. Tu peux me prêter un maillot?
(Yes, good idea. I really like it. Can you lend me some trunks?)

Grammar

Direct Object Pronouns

Don't be put off by the formal name, this is simply an easy way of saying "it" or "them" to save you from having to repeat a noun.

Compare these two sentences:

Tu aimes les frites? - Oui, j'aime les frites.   (Do you like chips? - Yes I like chips.)
Tu aimes les frites? - Oui, je les aime.   (Do you like chips? - Yes I like them.)

Notice the position in French le (it), la (it), les (them) AS A PRONOUN comes before the verb.

You also need to make your pronoun agree: le (masculine), la (feminine), l' (before a vowel), les (plural).

Study the examples:

Tu aimes le fromage? - Oui, je l'aime. Non, je le déteste. (Do you like cheese? - Yes, I like it. No, I hate it)
Tu aimes la bière? - Oui, je l'aime. Non je la déteste.   (Do you like beer? - Yes, I like it. No I hate it.)

Other pronouns you should know are; me, te, nous and vous (me, you, us and you).

These operate in the same way:
e.g.   Il m'aime   (he likes me)   il nous aime   (he likes us)
        Je te connais   (I know you)   Je vous connais (I know you.)

Foundation

Avez-vous un plan de la ville?
(Do you have a plan of the town?)
Oui, voilà.
(Yes, here you are.)

Est-ce qu'il y a une piscine près d'ici?
Est-ce qu'on peut faire de la natation ici?
(Is there a swimming pool nearby?
Can one go swimming here?)
Il y a une piscine dans la rue Pigny à deux
cents mètres d'ici.
(There is a swimming pool in the
Rue Pigny 200m from here.)

Je voudrais aussi une liste
de restaurants.
(I would also like a list of
restaurants.)
Oui, bien sûr. (Yes, of course.)

Et ça ferme à quelle heure?
(And it closes at what time?)
Le musée ferme à cinq heures.
(The museum closes at 5pm.)

Je cherche un horaire des autobus.
(I am looking for a bus timetable.)
Vous les trouverez là-bas.
(You will find them over there.)

Le musée, c'est ouvert tous les jours?
(Is the museum open every day?)
Tous les jours sauf le mardi.
(Every day except Tuesday.)

Pouvez-vous me donner
des renseignements sur les
monuments historiques/les musées?
(Can you give some information about
historic monuments/museums?)
Voici un dépliant sur les endroits
intéressants à visiter.
(Here is a leaflet on interesting places to visit.)

Est-ce qu'il y a des
excursions en car?
(Are there any coach trips?)
Il y a une excursion en car à
Paris le lundi. Départ Place du
Marché à 8 heures.
(There is a coach trip to Paris
on Mondays. Departure
from the Market
Square at 8am.)

Ça coûte combien?
(How much is that?)
C'est gratuit.
(It's free.)

Vocabulary

un Office de Tourisme/ un Syndicat d'Initiative	– Tourist Information Office	fermé(e)	– closed
un commissariat	– police station	sauf	– except
un panneau	– signpost	tous les jours (t.l.j.)	– every day
une liste	– a list	un jour de fête	– Bank Holiday
d'hôtels	– of hotels	un tarif	– price list
de campings	– of campsites	gratuit	– free
de chambres d'hôte	– of rooms	une réduction	– reduction
une carte	– a map	un groupe scolaire	– school party
un plan	– a plan	étudiant(e)	– student
un dépliant	– a leaflet	entrée libre	– free admittance
un horaire (des trains)	– a (train) timetable	une visite guidée	– guided tour
une excursion (en bateau)	– a (boat) trip	une distraction	– entertainment facility
à partir de	– from	louer	– to hire
ouvert(e)	– open	des cartes postales	– post cards

Higher

Note that the content here is very similar to Foundation Level but phrased in a more polite, sophisticated manner by using the conditional tense* (see grammar section below).

Est-ce qu'il serait* possible de louer un vélo pour la journée?
(Would it be possible to hire a bike for the day?)
Oui, il y a un magasin en ville qui loue des vélos.
(Yes, there is a shop in town which hires out bikes.)

Est-ce que vous pourriez* me donner un plan de la ville, s'il vous plaît?
(Could you give me a map of the town, please?)
Certainement, voilà Madame.
(Certainly, here you are.)

Est-ce que vous auriez* une carte de la région?
(Would you have a map of the area?)
Je regrette Madame, il n'en reste plus.
(I am sorry, Madam, there aren't any left.)

Je voudrais* savoir s'il y a un tarif réduit pour les groupes scolaires /les étudiants?
(Is there a reduction for school parties/students?)
Oui, mais seulement si vous avez une pièce d'identité.
(Yes, but only if you have an I.D. card).

Vous n'auriez* pas un horaire des trains par hasard?
(You wouldn't have a train timetable by any chance?)
Oui, bien sûr, Madame.
(Yes of course, Madam.)

Grammar

The Conditional Tense

Having learnt how to form the future tense will make the conditional seem easy. All you need to do is add IMPERFECT ENDINGS to the INFINITIVE or IRREGULAR FUTURE STEM.
The English translation always has "<u>would</u>" in it.

e.g. Je visiter<u>ais</u>	-	I would visit	Nous visiter<u>ions</u> - we would visit
Tu visiter<u>ais</u>	-	you would visit	Vous visiter<u>iez</u> - you would visit
Il/elle visiter<u>ait</u>	-	he/she would visit	Ils/elles visiter<u>aient</u> - they would visit

As with the future tense, -RE verbs lose the final -E before adding the endings.
E.g. prendre = to take, Je prendrais = I would take.

Note the following useful irregular verbs:

Je ferais	-	I would do/make	Je voudrais	-	I would like
J'irais	-	I would go	Je pourrais	-	I would be able to (I could)
Je serais	-	I would be	Je devrais	-	I should, ought to
J'aurais	-	I would have	Je viendrais	-	I would come
Je verrais	-	I would see			

Mini Test

1. Using "Je voudrais", ask for 10 different things that you could get from a Tourist Office.

2. Now think of 3 different ways of asking for the same things without using "Je voudrais".

3. Think of 5 other questions you may need to ask - e.g. prices, times, etc.

Foundation

Pouvez-vous m'aider? Je cherche le commissariat, s'il vous plaît.
(Can you help me? I'm looking for the police station, please.)
Descendez la Rue de l'Eglise, traversez le pont et c'est sur la place.
(Go down Church Road, cross the bridge and it's on the square.)

Où est la poste, s'il vous plaît Monsieur?
(Where is the post office, please Sir?)
Allez tout droit et c'est au bout de la rue.
(Go straight on and it's at the end of the road.)

Pour aller à l'Hôtel de la Gare, s'il vous plaît?
(How do I get to the Hotel de la Gare, please?)
Prenez la première rue à gauche, et puis la deuxième rue à droite.
(Take the first road on the left and then the second on the right.)

C'est loin la gare, Monsieur?
(Is it far to the station, Sir?)
Non, c'est à deux minutes à pied, allez tout droit et c'est en face de la banque.
(No, it's 2 minutes away on foot, go straight on and it's opposite the bank.)

Où se trouve la banque, s'il vous plaît?
(Where is the bank, please?)
Tournez à gauche au coin, traversez la place et c'est là.
(Turn left at the corner, cross the square and it's there.)

Il y a un bureau de change près d'ici, s'il vous plaît?
(Is there a bureau de change near here, please?)
Oui, c'est à deux cents mètres à gauche à côté du cinéma.
(Yes it's 200 metres away on the left next to the cinema.)

BANK

Vocabulary

allez tout droit	- go straight on		la rivière	- the river
c'est à gauche	- it's on the left		la rue	- the road
c'est à droite	- it's on the right		au carrefour	- at/to the crossroads
prenez la première/ deuxième/troisième rue	- take the first/second/third road		aux feux	- at/ to the traffic lights
			au rond-point	- at/to the roundabout
à droite	- on the right		*au bout de	- at the corner of
à gauche	- on the left		jusqu'à	- up to/as far as
traversez	- cross		*à côté de	- next to
suivez	- follow		*en face de	- opposite
descendez	- go down		sur	- on
montez	- go up		dans	- in
le pont	- the bridge		devant	- in front of
la place	- the square		derrière	- behind

Remember: Expressions followed by "de" follow the normal rules; (see page 83)

e.g.
à côté du cinéma	-	next to the cinema
à côtè de la banque	-	next to the bank
à côté de l'église	-	next to the church
à côté des toilettes	-	next to the toilets.

Higher

Je n'ai pas très bien compris. Pouvez-vous le répéter?
(I didn't understand very well. Can you repeat it?)
Pas de problème, vous suivez l'autoroute ...
(No problem, you follow the motorway ...)

Pour aller à la gare, est-ce que c'est mieux d'aller en autobus ou à pied?
(Is it better to go by bus or on foot to get to the station?)
C'est plus vite et plus facile de prendre l'autobus.
(It's quicker and easier to go by bus.)

SIGNAL AHEAD

Pardon Monsieur, je suis perdu. Pourriez-vous me donner des directions à Paris?
(Excuse me Sir, I'm lost. Could you give me directions to Paris?)
Oui, bien sûr, vous suivez l'autoroute jusqu'au bout et vous êtes là.
(Yes, of course, you follow the motorway to the end and you're there.)

Quelle est la meilleure route pour aller au marché, s'il vous plaît?
(What is the best route to get to the market, please?)
Il vaut mieux suivre cette rue jusqu'au bout et puis tourner à gauche.
(It's best to follow this road to the end and then turn left.)

Grammar

Imperatives

- If you are giving instructions or orders to someone formally you simply leave out the word for you (vous) and use the verb alone. All three groups (-ER, -RE and -IR) will end in -ez in this case.

e.g.
- allez - go
- prenez - take
- sortez - go out

- if you are giving instructions to a friend or relative, i.e. you are using "tu", the same format applies apart from -ER verbs where you need to drop the "s".

eg.
- va - go
- prends - take
- sors - go out

- Reflexive verbs need a reflexive pronoun after them in the imperative. (Instead of "te", use "toi")

eg.
- arrête-toi - stop!
- arrêtez-vous - stop!

- To make these commands negative, for the majority you can just surround them with NE and PAS.

e.g. ne va pas - don't go - n'allez pas
ne prends pas - don't take - ne prenez pas
ne sors pas - don't go out - ne sortez pas

for reflexive verbs the word order changes back to normal:
e.g. ne t'arrête pas - don't stop - ne vous arrêtez pas

Mini Test

1. Imagine that you are directing a French tourist around your town. Direct him from a hotel to **5** places he may need to go, e.g. bank, post office.

Foundation

Dans le métro
Pour aller à l'Arc de Triomphe, c'est quelle ligne, s'il vous plaît?
(To get to the Arc de Triomphe, which line is it, please?)
Il faut prendre la ligne numéro un direction Pont de Neuilly et vous descendez à Charles de Gaulle/Étoile.
(You need to take line 1 and you get off at Charles de Gaulle/Étoile.)

Dans l'autobus
Je voudrais aller à Royan. Est-ce qu'il y a un autobus?
(I'd like to go to Royan. Is there a bus?)
Oui, c'est la ligne numéro vingt.
(Yes, it's route 20.)

Le prochain bus part à quelle heure, s'il vous plaît?
(What time does the next bus leave, please?)
A onze heures. (At 11 o'clock.)

Le trajet dure combien de temps?
(How long does the journey last?)
A peu près quinze minutes.
(About 15 minutes.)

Dans le train
De quel quai part le train pour Royan?
(From which platform does the train to Royan leave?)
Il part du quai numéro quatre, voie numéro un.
(It leaves from platform 4 track 1.)

Ça coûte combien un aller simple pour un enfant et un aller-retour pour un adulte?
(How much is a single for a child and a return for an adult?)
Ça fait cinq Euros en tout.
(That'll be 5 Euros altogether.)

Est-ce que le bus s'arrête à la plage, ou est-ce que je dois changer?
(Does the bus stop at the beach or do I have to change?)
Il s'arrête à la plage, Madame.
(It stops at the beach, Madam.)

Remember: Many of these phrases are interchangeable for different means of transport.

Vocabulary

le bateau	-	boat	traverser	-	to cross
le ferry	-	ferry	le trajet	-	a journey
l'aéroglisseur	-	hovercraft	le voyage	-	a trip
l'hovercraft	-	hovercraft	le vol	-	flight
l'avion	-	aeroplane	le billet	-	ticket
le shuttle	-	shuttle	un carnet	-	book of 10 tickets (cheaper)
le tunnel	-	tunnel	un aller-retour	-	a return
le train	-	train	un aller-simple	-	a single
l'autobus	-	bus	première classe	-	first class
le car	-	coach	deuxième classe	-	second class
le transport en commun	-	public transport	fumeur	-	smoking
le moyen de transport	-	means of transport	non-fumeur	-	non-smoking
voyager	-	to travel	la gare	-	station
une station	-	a stop (underground)	la gare routière	-	bus station
un arrêt d'autobus	-	a bus stop	le port	-	port
une réservation	-	a reservation	l'aéroport	-	airport
départ	-	departure	SNCF	-	French Railways
arrivée	-	arrival	couchettes	-	sleeping compartments
descendre	-	to get off	en retard	-	late
monter	-	to get on	un délai	-	delay
durer	-	to last			

Higher

Est-ce qu'on devrait prendre l'autobus au lieu de la voiture?
(Should we travel by bus instead of by car?)
Je pense qu'on doit éviter d'utiliser la voiture en ville à cause de la pollution, mais c'est plus difficile à la campagne.
(I think that we should avoid using cars in town because of pollution, but it's more difficult in the countryside.)

Tu es allé(e) en France?
(Have you been to France?)
Oui, j'y suis allé(e) l'année dernière.
(Yes I went there last year.)

Comment as-tu voyagé?
(How did you travel?)
J'ai pris le bateau pour traverser la Manche parce que c'est moins cher et c'est pratique avec la voiture, et puis nous sommes descendus dans le Sud de la France.
(I took the boat to cross the Channel because it's cheaper and it's practical with a car, and then we drove to the South of France.)

Combien de temps a duré le voyage?
(How long did the trip last?)
Nous avons voyagé pendant environ 24 heures, c'était assez long mais nous nous sommes arrêtés deux ou trois fois pour manger.
(We travelled for around 24 hours, it was quite long but we stopped two or three times to eat.)

Grammar

Modal Verbs

You have already met Pouvoir (to be able to) when talking about things that you can do around town, see page 31 There are three more verbs which operate in a similar way.

1) **Vouloir - to want**
   Je veux - I want
   Tu veux - you want
   Il/elle veut - he/she wants
   nous voulons - we want
   vous voulez - you want
   Ils/elles veulent - they want

   e.g. Je veux un billet pour Paris, s'il vous plaît.
   I want a ticket to Paris, please.

2) **Devoir - to have to**
   Je dois - I have to
   Tu dois - you have to
   Il/elle doit - he/she has to
   nous devons - we have to
   vous devez - you have to
   Ils/elles doivent - they have to

3) **Savoir - to know (how to)**
   Je sais - I know
   Tu sais - you know
   Il/elle sait - he/she knows
   nous savons - we know
   vous savez - you know
   Ils/elles savent - they know

   e.g. Tu sais à quelle heure arrive le train?
   Do you know what time the train arrives?

   Remember: All of these verbs are followed by an infinitive:
   e.g. Je veux aller à Cognac.
   (I want to go to Cognac.)
   Je dois changer de train?
   (Do I have to change trains?)
   Je sais conduire.
   (I know how to drive.)

Foundation

<u>Un accident/(An accident)</u>
Attention! (Look out!)
Je suis désolé(e). Vous êtes blessé(e)?
(Oh, I'm very sorry. Are you hurt?)
J'ai mal à la jambe. (My leg hurts.)
Je vais téléphoner à la police et je vais
vous donner mon nom et mon adresse.
(I'm going to call the police and I'll give
you my name and address.)

<u>A la station-service/(At the Petrol Station)</u>
Faites le plein, s'il vous plaît.
(Fill the tank with petrol, please.)
Je voudrais quarante litres de super,
s'il vous plaît.
(I would like 40 litres of 4 star
petrol, please.)

<u>Au téléphone/(On the telephone)</u>
Je suis tombé(e) en panne sur
l'autoroute A26 en direction de Calais,
à dix kilomètres de St-Omer.
(I've broken down on the A26 motorway,
heading for Calais, 10 km from St-Omer.)
C'est quelle marque de voiture?
(What make of car is it?)
C'est une Ford Escort rouge,
numéro d'immatriculation JAZ 478X.
(It's a red Ford Escort, registration
number JAZ 478X.)
Vous pouvez envoyer un mécanicien?
(Can you send a mechanic?)
Oui, il faut attendre 40 minutes.
(Yes, you will have to
wait 40 minutes.)

Vous vendez des cartes de la région?
(Do you sell maps of the area?)
Oui, et aussi des boissons, des bonbons,
des journaux ...
(Yes, and we also sell drinks,
sweets, newspapers ...)

Pouvez-vous vérifier
l'huile/l'eau/les pneus,
s'il vous plaît?
(Can you check the
oil/water/tyres, please?)
J'ai tout vérifié.
Vous avez besoin d'huile.
(I've checked everything.
You need some oil.)

Vocabulary

l'essence	- petrol		marcher	- to go, work
super	- 4 star	e.g. le moteur ne marche pas	- the engine won't start
ordinaire	- 2 star		un pneu crevé	- a puncture
sans plomb	- lead free		être en panne sèche	- to run out of petrol
une carte de la région	- a map of the area		ça chauffe!	- it's getting hot! (engine)
vérifier	- to check		un bruit étrange	- a (strange) noise
la pression des pneus	- tyre pressure		la voiture	- car
l'eau	- water		la moto	- motor bike
l'huile	- oil		le scooter	- scooter
avoir besoin de	- to need		le camion	- lorry
nettoyer	- to clean		un accident	- accident
le pare-brise	- windscreen		un(e) blessé(e)	- an injured person
en panne	- broken down		téléphoner	- to telephone
les freins	- brakes		la police	- police
la batterie	- battery		une ambulance	- ambulance
le moteur	- engine		les sapeurs-pompiers	- fire service
le phare	- headlight		l'assurance	- insurance
les essuie-glaces	- windscreen wipers			

Higher

At Higher Level you will be expected to give, and to understand, more detailed information, particularly with regard to accidents.

J'allais en ville pour faire des achats. Je ne roulais pas vite.
(I was going into town to do some shopping. I wasn't driving fast.)
J'ai signalé, et j'ai changé de file, quand tout à coup, je suis entré(e) en collision avec une autre voiture. J'ai freiné, mais trop tard.
(I indicated, and changed lane, when suddenly I collided with another car. I braked, but too late.)
Ma voiture était un peu endommagée.
(My car was slightly damaged.)

Il y a eu un accident sur la Route Nationale 42.
(There has been an accident on the RN42.)
Qu'est-ce qui s'est passé? (What happened?)
Un camion roulait trop vite, et il a heurté une voiture qui débouchait d'une rue à droite et qui avait la priorité.
(A lorry was going too quickly, and hit a car coming out of a road on the right, which had right of way.)
Est-ce qu'il y a eu des blessés?
(Was anyone injured?)
L'automobiliste, qui ne portait pas de ceinture de sécurité, s'est cassé le bras.
(The motorist, who was not wearing his seat belt, suffered a broken arm.)

Higher Level Vocabulary

heurter	-	to collide, hit	signaler	-	to indicate
déboucher de	-	to emerge from, come out of	changer de file	-	to change lane
avoir la priorité	-	to have right of way	entrer en collision avec	-	to collide with, hit
une ceinture de sécurité	-	seat belt	freiner	-	to brake
conduire	-	to drive	endommagé(e)	-	damaged
rouler	-	to drive, move (of vehicle)	un feu rouge	-	a red light

Grammar

The Imperfect Tense

The Imperfect Tense is another past tense. It often translates the English "<u>was doing</u>",
e.g. Je roulais (imperfect) lentement quand une autre voiture m'a heurté(e).
     I was driving slowly when another car collided with me.

In the examples given on this page, the Imperfect describes the circumstances before the accident (how things were) and the perfect tense is used to describe what suddenly caused the accident.

To form the Imperfect tense, take the "nous" form of the present - nous roulons/we are driving. Remove the "nous" and the "ons" from the end of the verb and add the following endings:

je ...ais	nous ...ions	e.g. je conduisais	- I was driving
tu ...ais	vous ...iez	il roulait	- he was driving
il/elle ...ait	ils/elles ...aient	elle avait la priorité	- she had right of way
		ils ne portaient pas de ceinture de sécurité	- they were not wearing a seat belt

A few verbs form the imperfect stem in a different way, most notably the verb être. The Imperfect stem is ét-

      J'étais en retard   -   I was late
Les voitures étaient endommagées   -   the cars were damaged

Foundation

A la boulangerie/At the bakers
Quatre baguettes, s'il vous plaît.
(4 baguettes, please.)
Désolé, il n'en reste que trois.
(I'm sorry there are only 3 left.)
Bon, je les prends.
(Fine, I'll take them.)
J'ai seulement un billet de vingt Euros. Ça va?
(I've only got a 20 Euro note. Is that OK?)
Oui, ça va.
(Yes, that's fine.)

Au marché/At the market
Vous désirez?
(What would you like?)
C'est combien les fraises?
(How much are the strawberries?)
1 Euro, les 250 grammes.
(1 Euro for 250 grammes.)

A l'épicerie/At the grocer's
Je peux vous aider?
(Can I help you?)
Je voudrais deux bouteilles d'eau
minérale, s'il vous plaît.
(I would like 2 bottles of mineral
water, please.)
Vous voulez autre chose?
(Do you want anything else?)
Donnez-moi une boîte d'allumettes,
s'il vous plaît.
(Give me a box of matches, please.)

A la charcuterie/At the delicatessen
Avez-vous du pâté, s'il vous plaît?
(Do you have any pâté, please?)
Oui, combien en voulez-vous?
(Yes, how much would you like?)
J'en prends deux cents grammes.
Et je voudrais aussi six tranches de jambon.
(I'll take 200 grammes. And I would
also like 6 slices of ham.)

Vocabulary

un magasin	-	shop
un marché	-	market
une épicerie	-	grocer's
une charcuterie	-	delicatessen, pork butcher's
une boucherie	-	butcher's
une boulangerie	-	bakery
une crémerie	-	dairy
une pâtisserie	-	cake shop
un supermarché	-	supermarket
un hypermarché	-	hypermarket
les carottes	-	carrots
les champignons	-	mushrooms
un chou	-	cabbage
un chou-fleur	-	cauliflower
les haricots verts	-	green beans
une laitue	-	lettuce
un oignon	-	onion
les petits pois	-	peas
les pommes de terre	-	potatoes
les tomates	-	tomatoes
un ananas	-	pineapple
une banane	-	banana
un citron	-	lemon

les fraises	-	strawberries
les framboises	-	raspberries
un melon	-	melon
un pamplemousse	-	grapefruit
les pêches	-	peaches
les poires	-	pears
les pommes	-	apples
les raisins	-	grapes
le jambon	-	ham
le pâté	-	pâté
le pain	-	bread
une baguette	-	baguette, French stick
le fromage	-	cheese
le gâteau	-	cake
la tarte	-	flan
les biscuits	-	biscuits
les chips	-	crips
la confiture	-	jam
les oeufs	-	eggs
surgelés	-	frozen food
un chariot	-	shopping trolley
une bouteille consignée	-	bottle with returnable deposit

Higher

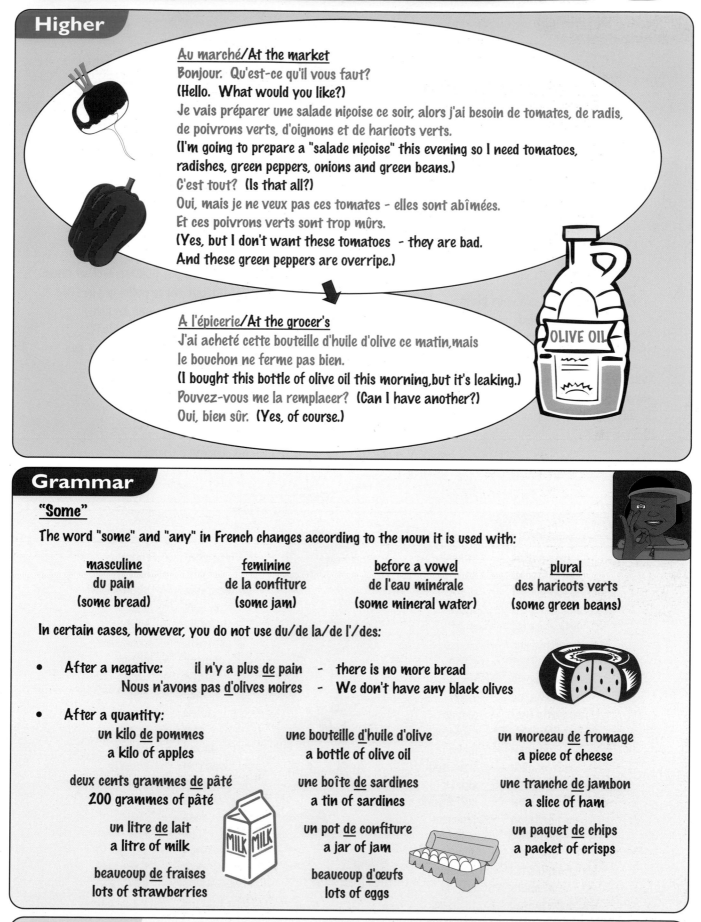

Au marché/At the market

Bonjour. Qu'est-ce qu'il vous faut?
(Hello. What would you like?)
Je vais préparer une salade niçoise ce soir, alors j'ai besoin de tomates, de radis, de poivrons verts, d'oignons et de haricots verts.
(I'm going to prepare a "salade niçoise" this evening so I need tomatoes, radishes, green peppers, onions and green beans.)
C'est tout? (Is that all?)
Oui, mais je ne veux pas ces tomates - elles sont abîmées.
Et ces poivrons verts sont trop mûrs.
(Yes, but I don't want these tomatoes - they are bad.
And these green peppers are overripe.)

A l'épicerie/At the grocer's

J'ai acheté cette bouteille d'huile d'olive ce matin, mais
le bouchon ne ferme pas bien.
(I bought this bottle of olive oil this morning, but it's leaking.)
Pouvez-vous me la remplacer? (Can I have another?)
Oui, bien sûr. (Yes, of course.)

OLIVE OIL

Grammar

"Some"

The word "some" and "any" in French changes according to the noun it is used with:

masculine	feminine	before a vowel	plural
du pain	de la confiture	de l'eau minérale	des haricots verts
(some bread)	(some jam)	(some mineral water)	(some green beans)

In certain cases, however, you do not use du/de la/de l'/des:

- After a negative: il n'y a plus <u>de</u> pain   -   there is no more bread
                 Nous n'avons pas <u>d'</u>olives noires   -   We don't have any black olives

- After a quantity:

un kilo <u>de</u> pommes	une bouteille <u>d'</u>huile d'olive	un morceau <u>de</u> fromage
a kilo of apples	a bottle of olive oil	a piece of cheese
deux cents grammes <u>de</u> pâté	une boîte <u>de</u> sardines	une tranche <u>de</u> jambon
200 grammes of pâté	a tin of sardines	a slice of ham
un litre <u>de</u> lait	un pot <u>de</u> confiture	un paquet <u>de</u> chips
a litre of milk	a jar of jam	a packet of crisps
beaucoup <u>de</u> fraises	beaucoup <u>d'</u>œufs	
lots of strawberries	lots of eggs	

Mini Test

1. Write out a shopping list, with quantities, of food needed to prepare your favourite meal (with starter, main course, dessert).

Foundation

Je voudrais essayer ces chaussures-là qui sont en vitrine.
(I'd like to try those shoes which are in the window.)
Bien sûr. Vous prenez quelle pointure?
(Of course. What is your shoe size?)

Je cherche un pull.
(I'm looking for a jumper.)
De quelle couleur?
(What colour?)
En bleu.
(In blue.)
Et vous faites quelle taille?
(And what size are you?)
Je fais du trente-huit.
(I'm a size 38.)

Avez-vous cette veste-ci en gris?
(Do you have this jacket in grey?)
Oui, voulez-vous l'essayer?
(Yes, do you want to try it on?)
... Je la prends
(... I'll take it.)
Payez à la caisse, s'il vous plaît.
(Pay at the cash desk, please.)

Nous avons ces pullovers-ci en rouge.
(We've got these pullovers in red.)
Vous ne les avez pas en bleu?
(Have you got them in blue?)
Je regrette, nous n'en avons pas.
(I'm sorry, we haven't.)

Vous avez quelque chose de plus grand?
(Have you got a bigger size?)
Je suis désolé(e), non.
(Sorry, no.)

Je peux essayer ce pantalon?
(Can I try these trousers on?)
Bien sûr. Les cabines d'essayage sont là-bas.
(Of course. The changing rooms are over there.)

Vocabulary

un anorak	-	anorak
un chapeau	-	hat
les chaussettes (f.)	-	socks
les chaussures (f.)	-	shoes
une chemise	-	shirt
un chemisier	-	blouse
un collant	-	tights
une cravate	-	tie
une écharpe	-	scarf
les gants (m.)	-	gloves
un imperméable	-	raincoat
un jean	-	jeans
un jogging	-	tracksuit
une jupe	-	skirt
un maillot de bain	-	swimming costume
un pantalon	-	trousers
un pull(over)	-	pullover
une robe	-	dress
les sandales (f.)	-	sandals
un short	-	shorts
les baskets (m.)	-	trainers
un tricot	-	cardigan
une veste	-	jacket
une cabine d'essayage	-	changing room
en coton	-	cotton
en laine	-	wool

en nylon	-	nylon
en cuir	-	leather
en plastique	-	plastic
en soie	-	silk
la taille	-	size
la pointure	-	shoe size
la couleur	-	colour
blanc	-	white
bleu	-	blue
brun	-	brown
gris	-	grey
jaune	-	yellow
marron	-	brown
noir	-	black
orange	-	orange
rose	-	pink
rouge	-	red
vert	-	green
bleu clair	-	light blue
bleu foncé	-	dark blue
bleu marine	-	navy blue

Rhinos

Remember: Colours are adjectives and must agree with the object they are describing. For information on adjective agreements and irregular adjectives, see pages **11** and **83**.

Higher

Je cherche un pullover rouge, taille 40.

(I'm looking for a red jumper, size 40.)

Nous avons plusieurs pulls en rouge; celui-ci est en laine, celui-là en acrylique.

(We have several pullovers in red; this one is woollen and this one is acrylic.)

Vous n'avez rien de moins cher? Non? Je peux utiliser une carte de crédit?

(Have you anything cheaper? No? Well, can I pay by credit card?)

Bien sûr.

(Of course.)

J'ai acheté cette robe hier; celle qui était en vitrine.

Il manque un bouton et il y a une tache à la manche. Vous pouvez me rembourser?

(I bought this dress yesterday; the one that was in the window. There's a button missing and a stain on the sleeve. Can I have a refund?)

Vous avez le reçu?

(Have you got the receipt?)

Oui? Alors pas de problème.

(Yes? Then there's no problem.)

Grammar

This, That, These, Those

If you want to point out a particular item or person, the different forms of "ce" are used as follows:

masculine	masculine before a vowel	feminine	plural
ce pull	cet imperméable	cette robe	ces chaussures
this pullover	this raincoat	this dress	these shoes

-ci or -là can be added to make it clearer exactly which you mean:

Vous préférez ce pantalon-ci ou ce pantalon-là?

Do you prefer this pair of trousers or that pair of trousers?

Je ne prends pas ces chausettes-ci.   Je prends ces chaussettes-là.

I won't take these socks.   I'll take those socks.

When "this" or "that" is <u>not</u> followed by a noun, celui, celle, ceux and celles are used to mean "the one(s)".

Again -ci or -là can be added to distinguish between "this one" and "that one":

masculine singular	feminine singular	masculine plural		feminine plural
celui-ci	celle-ci	ceux-ci	these	celles-ci
this one	this one			
celui-là	celle-là	ceux-là	those	celles-là
that one	that one			

Voici les deux robes. Celle-ci est en coton et celle-là est en soie.

Here are the 2 dresses. This one is cotton and that one is silk.

Vous préférez quels gants?   -   Je préfère ceux-ci en laine.

Which gloves do you prefer?   -   I prefer these in wool.

Foundation

Je cherche un cadeau pour mon frère. Il a 13 ans.
(I'm looking for a present for my brother. He's 13.)
Nous avons ces T-shirts-ci à prix réduit.
(We've got these T-shirts here at a reduced price.)

Dans un grand magasin/In a department store
Où se trouve le rayon d'alimentation, s'il vous plaît?
(Where is the food department, please?)
Au sous-sol.
(In the basement.)
Et pour les articles de sport?
(And for sports equipment?)
Au deuxième étage. Prenez l'ascenseur.
(On the 2nd floor. Take the lift.)

Il me faut un cadeau pour mes parents.
Qu'est-ce que vous me conseillez?
(I need a present for my parents. What can you suggest?)
Il y a cette boîte de chocolats à onze Euros ou cette boîte-là à dix-sept Euros.
(There's this box of chocolates for 11 Euros or that box for 17 Euros.)
Je prends celle-ci à 11 Euros, elle est moins chère. C'est pour offrir.
Pouvez-vous me faire un paquet-cadeau?
(I'll take this one for 11 Euros, it's cheaper. It's for a present. Can you gift-wrap it for me?)

Vous voulez payer comment?
(How do you want to pay?)
Vous acceptez les chèques de voyage?
(Do you accept travellers cheques?)
Bien sûr.
(Of course.)

Vocabulary

un grand magasin	- department store	un prix réduit	- reduced price
un rayon	- department	faire un paquet-cadeau	- to gift wrap
un rayon des disques	- record department	un cadeau	- a present
un rayon de sport	- sports department	une cassette	- cassette
un rayon d'alimentation	- food department	un CD	- CD
un rayon mode	- fashion/clothes department	un livre	- book
la parfumerie	- perfume department/shop	une boîte de petits gâteaux	- box/tin of biscuits
la bijouterie	- jewellery department/shop	une peluche	- soft toy
la librairie	- book department/shop	une poupée	- doll
la papeterie	- stationery department/shop	un porte-clés	- key ring
les vêtements	- clothes	un jeu de société	- board game
les jouets	- toys	une affiche	- poster
le ménage	- household goods	un chèque de voyage	- travellers' cheque
le rez-de-chaussée	- ground floor	une carte de crédit	- credit card
le sous-sol	- basement	la montre	- watch
le premier/deuxième étage	- 1st/2nd floor	rembourser	- to refund
la caisse	- till, cash desk	échanger	- to exchange (goods)
un ascenseur	- lift	chercher	- to look for
un escalier roulant	- escalator	conseiller	- to advise
une solde	- sale	faire du lèche-vitrine	- window shopping
un rabais	- discount		

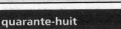

Higher

Je vous rapporte cette montre; je l'ai achetée hier et elle ne marche pas.
(I've brought this watch back; I bought it yesterday and it doesn't work.)
Vous l'avez achetée ici?
(Did you buy it here?)
Oui, voici le reçu.
(Yes, here's the receipt.)

Hier, je suis allé(e) en ville
pour acheter des cadeaux. D'abord j'ai cherché un cadeau pour ma mère. Je lui ai acheté du parfum. J'ai trouvé une chemise pour mon père; je l'ai vue dans la vitrine du magasin. J'ai cherché partout pour un cadeau pour mes frères jumeaux. Finalement je leur ai acheté du chocolat.
(Yesterday I went to town to buy some presents. First of all I looked for a present for my mum.
I bought some perfume for her. I found a shirt for my father; I saw it in the window of a
department store. I looked everywhere for a present for my twin brothers.
I finally bought some chocolate for them.)

Grammar

Me, You, Him, Her, Us, You, Them

You will find a note on these direct object pronouns on page 35. In the PERFECT TENSE they go BEFORE the AUXILIARY verb.

Voici <u>mon</u> pull. Je <u>l'</u>ai acheté hier. (masculine - mon pull)
(Here's my jumper. I bought it yesterday.)
Voici <u>ma</u> montre. Je <u>l'</u>ai achetée hier. (feminine - ma montre)
(Here's my watch. I bought it yesterday.)
Voici <u>mes</u> chaussures. Je <u>les</u> ai vues dans la vitrine. (feminine plural - mes chaussures)
(Here are my shoes. I saw them yesterday in the shop window.)

You will notice that in the above examples the PAST PARTICIPLE agrees with the DIRECT OBJECT when the latter comes IN FRONT OF THE VERB. This DIRECT OBJECT AGREEMENT can also occur with nouns, e.g.:

Voici <u>la</u> montre que j'ai achetée hier. (Here is the watch (which) I bought yesterday.)
Voici <u>les</u> chaussures que j'ai vues hier. (Here are the shoes (which) I saw yesterday.)

The same rule applies to me, te, nous and vous when used as a direct object.
Tu <u>nous</u> a vus en ville? (Did you see us in town?)

LUI and LEUR
Lui is a pronoun which replaces a masculine or feminine singular noun and usually means "to" or "for" him/her.
In the same way, LEUR replaces a plural noun and means "to" or "for" them.

Lui and Leur are INDIRECT OBJECT PRONOUNS.

J'ai acheté du chocolat (direct object) pour mes frères (indirect object).
(I bought some chocolate for my brothers).
Je leur (indirect object pronoun) ai acheté du chocolat.
(I bought some chocolate for them).

Foundation

Je voudrais envoyer ces cartes postales et ce colis en Suisse, s'il vous plaît.
(I'd like to send these postcards and this parcel to Switzerland, please.)
Il faut peser le colis. Ça fait quatre Euros au total.
(That'll be 4 Euros in total.)

A la banque/Au bureau de change
At the bank/At the bureau de change
Bonjour, monsieur, je voudrais toucher un chèque de voyage, s'il vous plaît.
(Hello, I'd like to cash a traveller's cheque, please.)
Bien sûr, avez-vous une pièce d'identité?
(Of course, have you got any I.D.?)

Je voudrais trois timbres à 56 cents, s'il vous plaît.
(I'd like 3 stamps at 56 cents, please.)

Oui, voilà mon passeport.
Quel est le taux de change, s'il vous plaît?
(Yes, here's my passport. What is the exchange rate, please?)
Aujourd'hui c'est 1,53 Euros, monsieur, vous voulez changer combien?
(It's 1,53 Euros to the pound today. How much would you like to change?)

A la poste/At the Post Office
Je voudrais envoyer une lettre en Angleterre, s'il vous plaît. C'est combien?
(I'd like to send a letter to England, please. How much is it?)
Ça fait 67 cents, s'il vous plaît.
(That will be 67 cents, please.)

Je voudrais changer cinquante livres sterling.
Est-ce qu'il faut payer une commission?
(I'd like to change £50. Do I have to pay commission?)
Oui, c'est 2%. Vous voulez signer ici, s'il vous plaît.
(Yes, it's 2%. Can you sign here, please.)

Vocabulary

l'argent	- money		un passeport	- a passport
les billets	- notes		une pièce d'identité	- I.D.
les pièces	- coins		un formulaire	- a form
les espèces	- cash		remplir	- to fill (in)
l'argent liquide	- cash		signer	- to sign
un chèque	- a cheque		envoyer	- to send
un chèque de voyage	- a traveller's cheque		peser	- to weigh
une carte de crédit	- a credit card		un paquet	- a packet
un eurochèque	- a Eurocheque		un colis	- a parcel
changer	- to change		une lettre	- a letter
toucher	- to cash		une carte postale	- a postcard
encaisser	- to cash		un timbre	- a stamp
le taux de change	- exchange rate		une boîte aux lettres	- a post box
la commission	- commission		Les P.T.T.	- Post Office

Higher

Money

Est-ce que c'est possible de toucher de l'argent en utilisant ma carte de crédit?
(Is it possible to withdraw money using my credit card?)
Oui, bien sûr, comment voulez-vous l'argent?
(Yes, of course, how would you like the money?)
Je voudrais cinq billets de vingt Euros et cinq billets de dix Euros, s'il vous plaît.
(I'd like 5 x 20 Euros and 5 x 10 Euros notes, please.)

Si j'envoie cette lettre aujourd'hui, quand est-ce qu'elle arrivera en Écosse?
(If I send this letter today , when will it arrive in Scotland?)
Normalement, ça prend trois jours mais malheureusement il y a une grève en ce moment, alors ça prendra plus longtemps.
(Normally it takes 3 days but unfortunately there is a strike at the moment so it will take longer.)

B A N K

Grammar

How to say 'To' a country or town

Use <u>À</u> with towns

e.g. Je voudrais envoyer cette lettre <u>à</u> Paris.
(I'd like to send this letter to Paris.)

use <u>EN</u> with countries (there are some exceptions - see below)

e.g. Je voudrais envoyer ce colis <u>en</u> Espagne.
(I'd like to send this parcel to Spain.)

Some common exceptions (masculine countries beginning with a consonant and all plurals):

e.g. <u>au</u> Portugal - to Portugal   <u>au</u> Japon - to Japan
      <u>au</u> Canada - to Canada   <u>aux</u> Etats-Unis - to the USA

Mini Test   (For pages 46 - 51)

1. Decide on **5** new items of clothing for your wardrobe. Imagine the conversations which would take place when buying them.

2. Write out a present list in French for members of your family and friends. Choose a different present for each person.

3. You are returning an item recently bought that you are unhappy with. Imagine the conversation.

4. Imagine yourself at the Bank/Post Office. Think of **5** questions you may need to ask in each place.

5. Look over numbers (page 6) and practise explaining how you would like your money.

Foundation

Location/Hiring

On peut louer des vélos?
(Can we hire bikes?)
Oui, monsieur, vous en voulez combien?
(Yes, sir, how many would you like?)
Deux vélos d'enfants, s'il vous plaît.
C'est combien par heure?
(Two children's bikes, please.
How much is it per hour?)
C'est 8 Euros par jour, et il y a une caution
de 16 Euros par vélo.
(It's 8 Euros a day and there is a
16 Euros deposit per bike.)

Le Bureau des Objets Trouvés
The Lost Property Office

Pouvez-vous m'aider, j'ai perdu ma
montre hier au buffet de à la gare?
(Can you help me, I lost my watch
yesterday in the station buffet?)
C'est comment?
(What is is like?)
Elle est petite, et noire et c'est une Rolex.
(It's small, it's black and it's a Rolex.)

Au pressing/At the dry cleaners

Est-ce qu'il y a un pressing près d'ici?
Je veux faire nettoyer ma robe.
(Is there a dry cleaner's near here?
I want to get my dress dry-cleaned.)
Il y en a un là-bas. Ça prendra un
jour et ça coûtera 8 Euros.
(There's one over there. It will take a
day and it will cost 8 Euros.)

Chez le photographe/At the camera shop

Pouvez-vous réparer mon appareil photo?
(Can you repair my camera?)
On va essayer.
(Maybe.)
Quand est-ce que ça sera prêt?
(When will it be ready?)
Demain.
(Tomorrow.)

Vocabulary

la location	-	hiring	égarer	-	to mislay
louer	-	to hire	faire (+ verb)	-	to get things done
un vélo	-	a bike	combien de temps?	-	How long?
une voiture	-	a car	longtemps	-	a long time
un bateau	-	a boat	prêt(e)	-	ready
une raquette	-	a racket	un appareil photo	-	a camera
le pressing	-	dry cleaner's	une pellicule	-	a film
le photographe	-	camera shop/photographer's	des lunettes	-	glasses
la bijouterie	-	jewellers	un collier	-	a necklace
réparer	-	to repair	une montre	-	a watch
nettoyer	-	to clean	un walkman	-	a walkman
développer	-	to develop	un manteau	-	a coat
casser	-	to break	décrire	-	to describe
perdre	-	to lose	dedans	-	inside
trouver	-	to find	le bureau des objets trouvés	-	lost property office
oublier	-	to forget			

Higher

Je voudrais louer une voiture pour la semaine, s'il vous plaît.
(I'd like to hire a car for the week, please.)
Pouvez-vous remplir ce formulaire, monsieur, et j'ai besoin de voir votre permis de conduire et une autre pièce d'identité?
(Can you fill in this form, Sir, and I need to see your driving licence and proof of identity?)
D'accord. Ça coûtera combien pour la semaine, y compris l'assurance?
(OK, how much will that be for the week, including the insurance?)

Je viens d'arriver et j'ai laissé mon sac à main dans le car. Pouvez-vous m'aider?
(I've just arrived and I've left my handbag on the coach. Can you help me?)
J'espère que oui, pouvez-vous le décrire?
(I hope so, can you describe it?)
Il est assez grand et il est en cuir, il est marron. Dedans il y a mes clés, mon porte-monnaie et mon passeport!
(It's quite big and it's made of leather, it's brown. Inside there are my keys, my purse and my passport!)

Je voudrais faire réparer mes lunettes, je les ai laissées tomber et le verre est cassé.
(I'd like to get my glasses repaired, I dropped them and the lens is broken.)
Je vais voir ce que je peux faire, monsieur, revenez demain vers trois heures.
(I'll see what I can do, Sir, come back tomorrow at around 3pm.)

Grammar

Getting Things Done

If you are making use of a particular service to get something done for you, you need to use "faire" + another infinitive verb.

e.g. 1) Je me fais <u>couper</u> les cheveux toutes les six semaines.
(I get my hair cut every six weeks.)

e.g. 2) Je vais <u>faire</u> <u>développer</u> mes photos.
(I'm going to get my photos developped.)

e.g. 3) Je dois <u>faire</u> <u>réparer</u> mon bracelet.
(I must get my bracelet repaired.)

Mini Test

1. Imagine you have lost your suitcase/handbag at the airport. Describe it and everything in it to an official.

2. Make a list of things you must get done before going on holiday.

Foundation

J'ai soif, tu veux boire quelque chose?
(I'm thirsty, do want a drink?)
Oui, d'accord, il y a un café là-bas.
(Yes, OK, there's a café over there.)

Vous avez quels parfums, monsieur?
(What flavours do you have?)
Nous avons des glaces à la vanille ou au chocolat.
(We've got vanilla or chocolate.)
Je prends une glace simple à la vanille, c'est combien?
(I'll have one scoop of vanilla, how much is it?)

Mesdames, qu'est-ce que vous prenez à boire?
(Ladies, what are you having to drink?)
Pour moi un orangina et pour elle un citron pressé.
(For me an orangina and for her a lemon juice.)

Maintenant j'ai chaud! Je vais prendre une glace.
(Now I'm hot! I'm going to get an ice-cream.)

Vous prenez quelque chose à manger?
(Are you having anything to eat?)
Oui, j'ai faim, je prends un sandwich au fromage et toi?
(Yes, I'm hungry, I'll have a cheese sandwich and you?)

On vous doit combien, monsieur?
(How much do we owe you?)
Ça fait douze Euros, s'il vous plaît.
(That will be 12 Euros, please.)

Qu'est-ce que vous avez comme pizza?
(What sort of pizzas do you have?)
Nous avons pizza au jambon ou aux champignons.
(We have ham or mushroom pizzas.)
Une pizza au jambon alors.
(A ham pizza, please.)

Vocabulary

la carte	-	menu
les casse-croûtes	-	snacks
les plats chauds	-	hot dishes
un sandwich	-	a sandwich
au pâté	-	with pâté
au jambon	-	with ham
une crêpe	-	a pancake
au beurre	-	with butter
au miel	-	with honey
aux oeufs	-	with eggs
à la chantilly	-	with cream
une salade	-	a salad
une glace	-	an ice-cream
au café	-	coffee (flavoured)
à la menthe	-	mint (flavoured)
à la pêche	-	peach (flavoured)
à la framboise	-	rasberry (flavoured)

à la fraise	-	strawberry (flavoured)
un croque-monsieur	-	cheese and ham toastie
une croque-madame	-	cheese and ham toastie with egg
des frites	-	chips
un café	-	(black) coffee
un café-crème	-	coffee with milk
un thé	-	a tea
un thé au lait	-	tea with milk
un thé au citron	-	lemon tea
un jus d'orange	-	orange juice
une bouteille d'eau minérale	-	a bottle of mineral water
gazeuse	-	fizzy
une bière	-	a beer
une pression	-	a draught beer
un verre de vin	-	a glass of wine
une limonade	-	a lemonade
un coca	-	a coke

Higher

> Qu'est-ce qu'on fait pour le déjeuner?
> **(What shall we do for lunch?)**
> Je n'ai que seize Euros, alors quelque chose qui ne coûte pas trop cher!
> **(I've only got 16 Euros so something not too expensive!)**

> Messieurs, qu'est-ce que vous prenez?
> **(Gentlemen, what are you having?)**
> Je voudrais un plat végétarien, qui est assez léger, s'il vous plaît.
> **(I'd like a vegetarian dish which is quite light, please.)**

> Tu veux essayer le restaurant que j'ai vu là-bas?
> **(Do you want to try the restaurant that I saw over there?)**
> Je préfère en chercher un autre qui a plus de choix pour les végétariens, en plus celui-là avait l'air un peu cher.
> **(I prefer to look for another which has more choice for vegetarians, what's more that one looked a bit expensive.)**

> D'accord, on peut regarder dans mon guide de Paris et tu peux me dire lequel tu préfères. Il y en a plusieurs.
> **(OK, we can look in my Paris guide and you can tell me which one you prefer. There are several of them.)**
> Ça te dirait d'aller au "café végétarien", il paraît bon marché?
> **(Would you fancy going to the "Vegetarian Café", it looks like good value?)**

Grammar

Relative Pronouns QUI and QUE

Qui and Que mean who, whom, which and that. Both can be used to refer to people and things. Qui and Que introduce a relative clause which makes your sentence longer and more complex. Compare these two sentences:

e.g. 1) Le garçon travaille au café. Il est beau.
     (The waiter works in the café. He is good-looking.)

e.g. 2) Le garçon qui travaille au café est beau.
     (The waiter who works in the café is good-looking.)

Which one to use?

If it is the subject of the verb that follows it use "<u>qui</u>":
eg. Le garçon <u>qui</u> me sert. (The waiter <u>who</u> is serving me.)
i.e. in practice "<u>qui</u>" is normally followed by a verb (sert).

If it is the object of the verb that follows it use "<u>que</u>":
e.g. Le garçon <u>que</u> j'ai vu l'autre jour. (The waiter who I saw the other day.)
i.e. in practice "<u>que</u>" is normally followed by a noun or pronoun (je) then the verb.

Mini Test

1. Order snacks, drinks and ice creams for a group of 4 people.

Foundation

L'addition, s'il vous plaît.
(The bill, please.)
Voilà monsieur.
(Here you are sir.)
Le service est compris?
(Is service included?)
Oui monsieur.
(Yes sir.)

Une table pour quatre, s'il vous plaît.
(A table for 4, please.)
Oui, monsieur, à côté de la fenêtre, ça vous va?
(Yes, sir, next to the window, will that do for you?)
Parfait. (Perfect.)

Le menu, s'il vous plaît.
(The menu, please.)
Voilà, nous avons aussi un menu du jour.
(There you are, we also have a daily menu.)

Et comme boisson, monsieur?
(And to drink, sir?)
Qu'est-ce que vous recommandez?
(What do you recommend?)
Je recommande le Beaujolais nouveau, il est très bon.
(I recommend the Beaujolais nouveau, it's very good.)
Alors une bouteille de Beaujolais nouveau.
(A bottle of Beaujolais nouveau then.)

Qu'est-ce que vous prenez comme hors-d'œuvres?
(What would you like as a starter?)
Pour moi, le pâté.
(For me, the pâté.)

Et comme plat principal?
(And for the main course?)
Je prends le poulet rôti avec des haricots verts.
(I'll have the roast chicken with green beans.)

Et comme dessert? (And for dessert?)
Qu'est-ce que c'est le clafoutis? (What is "clafoutis"?)
C'est une sorte de tarte aux cerises. (It's a sort of cherry tart.)
Alors je prends ça. (I'll have that then.)

Vocabulary

le menu	-	menu	un digestif	- a drink after meal
le menu du jour	-	menu of the day	un couteau	- a knife
le plat du jour	-	dish of the day	une fourchette	- a fork
hors-d'œuvres	-	starters	une cuillère	- a spoon
le plat principal	-	main course	une assiette	- a plate
potages	-	soups	un bol	- a bowl
poissons	-	fish	un verre	- a glass
viandes	-	meat	le garçon/le serveur	- waiter
légumes	-	vegetables	le boeuf	- beef
desserts	-	desserts	le porc	- pork
boissons	-	drinks	l'agneau	- lamb
service compris	-	service included	les côtelettes	- cutlets
service non compris	-	service not included	le poulet	- chicken
en sus	-	extra	le saumon	- salmon
un pourboire	-	a tip	la truite	- trout
l'addition	-	the bill	les cuisses de grenouille	- frog's legs
un couvert	-	a place setting	les escargots	- snails
un apéritif	-	a drink before meal		

Higher

Vous avez aimé les escargots, madame?
(Did you like the snails, Madam?)
Non, je les ai trouvés assez durs.
(No, I found them quite tough.)
Je regrette, madame, qui vous
les a recommandés?
(I'm sorry, Madam, who recommended
them to you?)
Le garçon me les a recommandés.
(The waiter recommended them to me.)
On peut vous offrir un digestif?
Un cognac peut-être?
(Can we offer you a digestif?
Maybe a cognac?)
Merci, je ne l'aime pas non plus!
(No thanks, I don't like that either!)

Le cassoulet est très bon, madame.
(The cassoulet is very good, Madam.)
Qu'est-ce que c'est exactement?
Qu'est-ce qu'il y a dedans?
(What is it exactly? What's in it?)
C'est une sorte de ragoût, c'est fait
avec du lard, du saucisson, des haricots
blancs et des tomates et de l'ail.
C'est délicieux!
(It's a sort of stew made with bacon,
sausage, beans and tomatoes and
garlic. It's delicious!)
Je suis végétarienne alors je
ne mange pas de viande!
(I'm vegetarian so I don't
eat meat!)

Grammar

Order of Pronouns

Object pronouns go before the verb but have a special order if there is more than one of them. Follow this table:

me	le			
te	la	lui		
nous	l'		y	en
vous	les	leur		

e.g. Le garçon <u>me le</u> recommande. (The waiter recommends it to me.)

Notice the position of object pronouns in the perfect tense.
e.g. Le garçon <u>me</u> l'a recommandé. (The waiter recommended it to me.)

Also notice the word order with negatives where <u>NE</u> and <u>PAS</u> surround the object pronouns and the verb/auxiliary verb:
e.g. Le garçon <u>ne</u> me le recommande <u>pas</u>. (The waiter doesn't recommend it to me.)
e.g. Le garçon <u>ne</u> me l'a <u>pas</u> recommandé. (The waiter didn't recommend it to me.)

The order is slightly different in positive commands; direct object pronouns come before indirect object pronouns. <u>Y</u> and <u>EN</u> come last.

e.g. Donne-le moi! (Give it to me!)
     Donne m'en! (Give me some!)

Mini Test

1. List as many items of food and drink as you can in the form of a menu. Using the menu you have made order yourself a 3 course meal.

Foundation

Il n'y a pas assez de cintres,
l'oreiller est sale et la douche ne marche pas!
(There aren't enough coathangers, the
pillow is dirty and the shower doesn't work!)
On va régler ça tout de suite.
(We'll sort it out straight away.)

Je voudrais réserver une chambre à
deux personnes, s'il vous plaît.
(I'd like to reserve a double room, please.)
Oui, c'est à quel nom?/ Au nom de HILL.
(Yes, what's the name?/ The name is HILL.)

A quelle heure est-ce que le petit
déjeuner est servi?
(What time is breakfast served?)
De sept heures à dix heures dans la
salle à manger.
(from 7 to 10 in the dining room.)

Vous voulez une chambre
avec salle de bains ou avec douche?
(Do you want a room with a bathroom or a shower?)
Avec salle de bains, s'il vous plaît,
et aussi avec un balcon.
(With a bathroom, please and
also with a balcony.)

Vous avez la clé?
(Have you got the key?)
Oui, voilà, c'est la chambre vingt-cinq au deuxième étage.
(Yes, here you are, it's room 25 on the 2nd floor.)

C'est pour combien de nuits?
(How many nights is it for?)
C'est pour cinq nuits.
(It's for 5 nights.)

D'accord, c'est combien?
(OK, how much is it?)
C'est cent soixante Euros en tout avec
le petit déjeuner.
(It's 160 Euros in all with breakfast.)

Le petit déjeuner est compris?
(Is breakfast included?)
Non, il faut payer un supplément de trois Euros.
(No, you have to pay 3 Euros extra.)

Vocabulary

une chambre	-	a room	la clé	-	key
à une personne	-	for one person	complet	-	full
libre	-	free	le savon	-	soap
un lit à une personne	-	a single bed	la serviette	-	towel
un lit à deux personnes	-	a double bed	le robinet	-	tap
un drap	-	a sheet	la réception	-	reception
une couverture	-	a blanket	l'ascenseur	-	lift
un oreiller	-	a pillow	l'escalier	-	stairs
un balcon	-	a balcony	le couloir	-	corridor
avec vue sur la mer	-	with a seaview	une nuit	-	a night
avec salle de bains	-	with bathroom	coûter	-	to cost
avec douche	-	with a shower	compris	-	included
avec lavabo	-	with a washbasin	un supplément	-	extra
avec W.C.	-	with toilet	la pension complète	-	full board
au rez-de-chaussée	-	on the ground floor	la demi pension	-	half board
			faire une réservation	-	to make a reservation
au { premier / deuxième / troisième } étage	-	on the { 1st floor / 2nd floor / 3rd floor }	réserver	-	to reserve
			une étoile	-	star

Higher

Au téléphone/**On the telephone**
Allô, est-ce que c'est l'Hôtel de la Gare?
(Hello is that the Station Hotel?)
Oui, monsieur, comment puis-je vous aider? **(Yes, sir, how can I help you?)**
Je voudrais savoir s'il vous reste des chambres pour deux personnes du 16 août au 31 août?
(I'd like to know if you have any rooms left from the 16th August to the 31st August?)
Il ne nous reste qu'une chambre, monsieur. **(We only have one room left, sir.)**
Très bien, je la prends, s'il vous plaît.
(Very good, I'll take it please.)

Je voudrais me plaindre de l'état de ma chambre.
(I'd like to make a complaint about the state of my room.)
Quel est le problème, monsieur?
(What is the problem, sir?)
Il y en a plusieurs et j'en ai marre, à chaque fois que
j'y retourne il y a encore un problème. Aujourd'hui
c'est le robinet qui coule tout le temps.
**(There are several of them and I'm fed up, every time
I go back there, there's another problem.
Today it's the tap which keeps dripping.)**

Grammar

Y and EN

These two pronouns are quite common. As with other pronouns they go in front of the verb.

Y

"Y" usually means "there". e.g. J'y vais tous les ans. (I go there every year.)

It also appears in set expressions such as "il y a ..." (there is/are)
and can be tagged on to orders to encourage action, e.g. vas-y! allez-y! (Go on!)

EN

"En" usually means "of it, of them, some or any".
e.g. J'en ai (I've got some) Je n'en ai pas (I haven't got any)

Il reste des chambres? (Are there any rooms left?)
Oui, il en reste deux. (Yes, there are 2 (of them) left.)

Mini Test

1. Book yourself into a luxury room with at least 5 facilities.

2. Imagine yourself in the worst hotel room ever and report all its faults to reception.

Foundation

Est-ce que c'est possible
de prendre des repas ici?
(Is it possible to have meals here?)
Oui, vous pouvez acheter un repas dans
la salle à manger ou vous pouvez faire
de la cuisine vous-mêmes.
(Yes you can buy a meal
in the dining room or you
can cook for yourselves.)

Au camping/At the campsite
Vous avez de la place pour une
caravane et une tente, s'il vous plaît?
(Have you got room for a caravan
and a tent, please?)
Oui, c'est pour combien de nuits?
(Yes, for how many nights?)
Pour une nuit seulement.
(Just for one night.)

Vous êtes combien?
(How many are there of you?)
Nous sommes deux adultes et deux enfants.
(There are 2 adults and 2 children.)

A l'auberge de Jeunesse/At the Youth Hostel
Vous avez des places libres pour une fille et
deux garçons?
(Have you got room for a girl and 2 boys?)
Oui, le dortoir des filles est à gauche et le
dortoir des garçons est au premier étage.
(Yes, the girls' dormitory is on the left and
the boys' dormitory is on the 1st floor.)

Quel est votre numéro d'immatriculation?
(What is your registration number?)
C'est JSM 33.
(It is JSM 33.)

Voilà, c'est l'emplacement
numéro trente à côté du bloc sanitaire.
(There you are, it's pitch number 30 next
to the shower block.)

Qu'est-ce qu'il y a au camping?
(What is there on the campsite?)
Il y a une prise d'eau pour caravanes et un branchement électrique.
(There is a water and electricity point for caravans.)

Vocabulary

le camping	-	campsite	les plats cuisinés	-	ready cooked meals (take-away)
l'auberge de jeunesse	-	youth hostel	la prise d'eau	-	water point
une tente	-	a tent	le branchement électrique	-	power point
une caravane	-	a caravan	les équipements	-	facilities
un dortoir	-	dormitory	ouvert toute l'année	-	open all year round
une place	-	a space	le logement	-	accommodation
un emplacement	-	a pitch	un sac de couchage	-	sleeping bag
la laverie	-	laundry	le camping-gaz	-	camping gas
le bloc sanitaire	-	shower block	des allumettes	-	matches
la salle de repassage	-	ironing room	le bureau d'accueil	-	reception office
la salle de télévision	-	TV room	les poubelles	-	dustbins
la salle de jeux	-	games room	le terrain de pétanques		
l'alimentation	-	food	boules	} -	bowls area
			le parking	-	car park

Higher

Quelles sont les règles ici à l'auberge de jeunesse?
(What are the rules here at the youth hostel?)
Eh bien, la porte est fermée à clé à minuit. Vous devez parler doucement dans les dortoirs après dix heures du soir. Enfin il est strictement interdit d'utiliser le camping-gaz dans l'auberge.
(Well, the door is locked at midnight. You must speak quietly after 10pm. Finally it is strictly forbidden to use camping-gas in the hostel.)

Monsieur, je viens régulièrement à ce camping mais cette année je ne suis pas du tout satisfait de notre emplacement.
(Sir, I come to this campsite regularly but this year I'm not at all satisfied with our pitch.)
Pour quelles raisons, monsieur?
(For what reasons, sir?)
Tout d'abord, la prise d'eau ne marche pas, notre emplacement manque d'ombre et quelqu'un a cassé une fenêtre de notre caravane!
(First of all the water doesn't work, there's a lack of shade on our pitch and someone has broken a window in our caravan!)

Grammar

Adverbs

Adverbs usually describe verbs but can also be added to adjectives or other adverbs to give you more information. They may also stand alone. Adverbs do not need to agree.

e.g. Tu viens en France régulièrement?
(Do you come to France regularly?)

Formation of adverbs

- to form an adverb from an adjective you need to take the feminine form and add -ment:
e.g. finale - finalement (finally), douce - doucement (softly, quietly)

- if the masculine form ends in a vowel you simply add -ment to it:
e.g. poli - poliment (politely)

- There are some exceptions such as adjectives ending in -ent or -ant, which form adverbs ending in -emment and -amment:
e.g. patient - patiemment (patiently)
     courant - couramment (currently)

Some adjectives can be used as adverbs without changing them:
e.g. vite (fast) - parler vite (to speak quickly)

Others include: dur (hard), bas (low, quiet), fort (strong, loud)

Important irregular adverbs include: peu (little), bien (well), mieux (better), moins (less), mal (badly)

Foundation

Si ça ne va pas mieux dans deux jours, il faut consulter le médecin.
(If you are no better in 2 days, you need to see the doctor.)

Chez le pharmacien/At the chemist's
Je ne me sens pas bien. Je suis très enrhumé(e).
Vous pouvez me donner quelque chose?
(I don't feel well. I've got a bad cold.
Can you give me something?)
Oui. Vous pouvez prendre de l'aspirine, et nous avons des pastilles pour la gorge.
(Yes you can take aspirin and we have throat sweets.)

Ça fait combien?
(How much is it?)
Ça fait six Euros.
(It's 6 Euros)
Je peux avoir un reçu?
(Can I have a receipt?)

Avez-vous quelque chose contre la diarrhée?
(Do you have anything for diarrhoea?)
Ce médicament est très bon.
(This medicine is very good.)

Je voudrais quelque chose pour la toux.
(I would like something for my cough.)
Prenez ce sirop deux fois par jour.
(Take this cough mixture twice a day.)

Vocabulary

Le Corps Humain – The Body

le visage (face)
la gorge (throat)
le bras (arm)
la main (hand)
les doigts (fingers)
le pouce (thumb)
le genou (knee)
le pied (foot)

la tête (head)
le cou (neck)
la poitrine (chest)
le coude (elbow)
le ventre/l'estomac (m) (stomach)
la cuisse (thigh)
la jambe (leg)
la cheville (ankle)
les orteils/doigts de pied (toes)

le front (forehead)
les yeux (eyes)
l'œil (eye)
la joue (cheek)
le menton (chin)
le sourcil (eyebrow)
l'oreille (f.) (ear)
le nez (nose)
la bouche (mouth)

Also:

l'épaule (f.)	-	shoulder
le dos	-	back
la taille	-	waist
le poignet	-	wrist
le talon	-	heel
la lèvre	-	lip
la dent	-	tooth
la langue	-	tongue

la pharmacie	-	chemist's
le pharmacien	-	chemist, pharmacist
je suis enrhumé(e)	-	I've got a cold
se couper le doigt	-	to cut one's finger
se tordre la cheville	-	to sprain one's ankle
la diarrhée	-	diarrhoea
la toux	-	cough
une piqûre d'insecte	-	an insect bite

un médicament	-	medicine
un sirop	-	cough mixture
un pansement	-	bandage
un sparadrap	-	plaster
les pastilles	-	throat sweets
l'aspirine	-	aspirin
une crème antiseptique	-	antiseptic cream

Higher

Chez le pharmacien/At the chemist's
J'ai été piqué(e) par une guêpe. Pouvez-vous me conseiller quelque chose?
(I've been stung by a wasp. Can you recommend something?)
Je peux vous donner une crème.
(I can give you some cream.)

Je me suis coupé le doigt. Qu'est-ce que vous pouvez me proposer?
(I've cut my finger. What do you suggest I do?)
Je peux vous donner un sparadrap.
(I can give you a plaster.)

Je crois que je me suis tordu la cheville - pouvez-vous me mettre un bandage?
(I think I've sprained my ankle - can you bandage it up?)
Oui, bien sûr.
(Yes, of course.)

Grammar

Reflexive Verbs with Parts of the Body

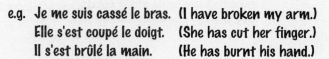

Remember that a REFLEXIVE VERB indicates something that you do to or for yourself. When discussing illnesses and ailments, it is most likely you will be using a reflexive verb with a part of the body in the PERFECT TENSE.

e.g. Je me suis cassé le bras.   (I have broken my arm.)
Elle s'est coupé le doigt.   (She has cut her finger.)
Il s'est brûlé la main.   (He has burnt his hand.)

<u>Se casser la jambe - to break one's leg!</u>

Je me suis cassé la jambe	-	I have broken/did break my leg
Tu t'es cassé la jambe	-	You have broken/did break you leg
Il/elle s'est cassé la jambe	-	He/she has broken/did break his/her leg.

When a reflexive verb is used in the perfect tense with a part of the body in this way, the past participle does NOT change to agree with the feminine or plural subject, eg:

<u>elle</u> s'est brûlé_ la main.   (She burnt her hand.)

However when a reflexive verb which makes no reference to a part of the body, e.g. se lever (to get up), se coucher (to go to bed) is used in the perfect tense, it is necessary to make the past participle agree with the subject as follows:

Je me suis levé(e) de bonne heure	-	I got up early
Tu t'es levé(e) de bonne heure	-	you got up early
Il s'est levé_ de bonne heure	-	he got up early
Elle s'est levée de bonne heure	-	she got up early
Nous nous sommes levé(e)s de bonne heure	-	we got up early
Vous vous êtes levé(e)(s) de bonne heure	-	you got up early
Ils se sont levés de bonne heure	-	they got up early (male or mixed group)
Elles se sont levées de bonne heure	-	they got up early (female group)

NB: possible feminine or plural forms given in brackets.

Foundation

Chez le dentist/At the dentist's
J'ai mal aux dents. J'ai perdu un plombage il y a deux jours.
(I've got toothache. I lost a filling 2 days ago.)
Laissez-moi voir. Oui, je vais la replomber tout de suite.
(Let me see. Yes, I'll give you another filling straight away.)
Vous voulez une piqûre?
(Would you like an injection?)
Oui, s'il vous plaît.
(Yes, please.)

Au téléphone/On the telephone
Je voudrais prendre un rendez-vous avec le médecin/le dentiste.
(I would like to make an appointment with the doctor/dentist.)
Pouvez-vous venir demain à deux heures?
Votre nom, s'il vous plaît?
(Can you come tomorrow at 2pm? Your name, please?)

Chez le médecin/At the doctor's
J'ai mal au ventre et j'ai de la fièvre depuis trois jours.
(I've had stomach ache and a temperature for 3 days.)
Ce n'est pas grave. Je vais vous donner une ordonnance.
Prenez ces comprimés après les repas et restez au lit.
(It's not serious. I'll give a prescription. Take this medicine after meals and stay in bed.)

Chez le médecin(2)/At the doctor(2)
Qu'est-ce qui ne va pas?
(What seems to be the matter?)
J'ai mal au genou.
(My knee hurts.)
Laissez-moi voir. Ça vous fait mal?
(Let me see. Does that hurt?)
Oui, ça me fait mal.
(Yes, that hurts.)
Il faut vous reposer.
(You need to rest.)

Vocabulary

J'ai mal à la tête	-	I've got a headache	grave	- serious
J'ai mal à la gorge	-	sore throat	douloureux	- painful
J'ai mal au ventre	-	stomach ache	un rendez-vous	- appointment
J'ai mal au coeur	-	I feel sick	les heures de consultation	- surgery hours
J'ai mal aux dents	-	toothache	les comprimés	- tablets
J'ai de la fièvre	-	I've got a temperature	une ordonnance	- a prescription
un coup de soleil	-	sunburn	j'ai perdu l'appétit	- I've lost my appetite
un rhume	-	a cold	un plombage	- a filling
un rhume des foins	-	hay fever	replomber	- to refill (tooth)
la grippe	-	flu	une piqûre	- an injection
avoir soif/faim	-	to be thirsty/hungry	se casser la jambe	- to break one's leg
avoir chaud/froid	-	to be hot/cold	se brûler la main	- to burn one's hand
vomir	-	to vomit	se déchirer un muscle	- to tear a muscle
se faire mal	-	to hurt oneself	se tordre le poignet	- to sprain one's wrist
examiner	-	to examine	l'asthme	- asthma
traiter	-	to treat	une allergie (à)	- an allergy (to)
se reposer	-	to rest	allergique (à)	- allergic (to)

Higher

Chez le médecin (1)/At the doctor's (1)
Je me suis déchiré un muscle en
jouant au foot.
(I've torn a muscle playing football.)
C'est très douloureux?
(Is it very painful?)
Oui, je n'ai pas dormi de la nuit.
(Yes, I've not been able to sleep at night.)
Il faut bouger le moins possible et vous
devez mettre un pansement.
**(You must try to move as little
as possible, and bandage it up.)**

Chez le médecin (2)/At the doctor's (2)
Je me suis brûlé la main en faisant la cuisine.
(I've burnt my hand whilst cooking.)
Faites voir votre main. Comment avez-vous
fait ça exactement?
**(Let me see your hand. How did you do that
exactly?)**
En versant de l'eau bouillante dans une casserole.
(Whilst pouring boiling water into a pan.)
Il faut aller directement à l'hôpital.
(You must go straight to hospital.)

Grammar

EN and PRESENT PARTICIPLE – whilst doing something...

The present participle of a verb translates the English expression "<u>whilst</u>" or "<u>by doing something</u>".
It is formed by taking the 'nous' form of the verb in the PRESENT TENSE, deleting ONS and adding
ANT as follows:

Nous jouons (we play)   ~~nous jouons~~   en jouant   -   whilst playing

Nous faisons du sport   ~~nous faisons~~   en faisant du sport   -   whilst playing/doing some sport

Nous mangeons   ~~nous mangeons~~   en mangeant   -   whilst eating (NB extra "e" to make a soft "g")

Two important exceptions are:
être   étant   -   being
avoir   ayant   -   having

Mini Test

1. List as many parts of the body as you can in French in one minute.

2. Imagine a conversation with a chemist in French, in which you describe 3 ailments.
   What remedies could be offered?

Foundation

Que penses-tu de la drogue?
(What is your opinion of drugs?)
La drogue, c'est dangereuse. Il y a beaucoup de risques pour la santé.
(Drugs are dangerous. There are many risks to one's health.)

Tu es sportif/sportive?
(Are you sporty?)
Oui, je fais du sport trois fois par semaine.
(Yes, I do some sport 3 times a week.)

Tu bois de l' alcool?
(Do you drink alcohol?)
Je bois de la bière de temps en temps.
(I occasionally have a beer.)

Qu'est-ce qu'il faut manger et boire pour être sain?
(What should one eat and drink to stay healthy?)
Il faut manger beaucoup de fruits et de légumes et boire de l'eau.
(One should eat lots of fruits and vegetables and drink water.)

Tu fumes?
(Do you smoke?)
Je ne fume jamais. Le tabac, c'est malsain.
(I never smoke. Tobacco is bad for your health.)

Qu'est-ce qu'il ne faut pas manger/boire?
(What should one not eat/drink?)
Il ne faut pas manger trop de bonbons. On ne doit pas boire trop de café.
(You shouldn't eat too many sweets or drink too much coffee.)

Tu te couches à quelle heure?
(What time do you go to bed?)
Je me couche assez tôt pendant la semaine.
(I go to bed quite early during the week.)

Vocabulary

la santé	-	health	éviter	-	to avoid
sain/bon pour la santé	-	healthy	les sucreries	-	sweet things
malsain/mauvais pour la santé	-	unhealthy	les graisses	-	fatty foods
			la viande	-	meat
faire de l'exercice	-	to exercise	végétarien(ienne)	-	vegetarian
le tabac	-	tobacco	se détendre/se relaxer	-	to relax
l'alcool	-	alcohol	les problèmes de l'adolescence	-	youth/teenager's problems
la drogue	-	drugs			
dangereux(euse)	-	dangerous	le stress	-	stress
dégoûtant(e)	-	disgusting	les boutons	-	spots
de temps en temps	-	from time to time	la dépression	-	depression
avec modération	-	with moderation	déprimé(e)	-	depressed
régulièrement	-	regularly	la fatigue	-	tiredness
rarement	-	rarely	l'appétit	-	appetite
tôt	-	early	la dépendance	-	dependancy
tard	-	late	le risque	-	risk
être en forme	-	to be fit and healthy	la maladie	-	illness
se maintenir en forme	-	to keep fit			

Higher

> Qu'est-ce que tu fais pour te maintenir en forme? Je fais régulièrement de l'exercice - la natation, le yoga, la danse et je mange bien.
> **(I exercise regularly - swimming, yoga, dance and I eat well.)**

> Quels sont les risques de prendre de la drogue?
> **(What are the risks of taking drugs?)**
> La dépendance, et pour ceux qui s'injectent, le risque du Sida.
> **(Dependancy, and for those who inject, the risk of Aids.)**

> Qu'est-ce que ça veut dire "bien manger"?
> **(What does that mean "eat well"?)**
> Je ne mange pas beaucoup de viande et j'essaie d'éviter les sucreries et les graisses.
> **(I don't eat much meat and I try to avoid sweet things and fatty food.)**

> Pourquoi est-ce qu'on fume/boit de l'alcool?
> **(Why do people smoke/drink alcohol?)**
> Par curiosité ou parce qu'on pense que c'est chic ou que ça fait adulte.
> **(Out of curiosity or because people think it's chic or "grown up".)**

> Qu'est-ce que tu fais pour te détendre?
> **(What do you do to relax?)**
> Pour me relaxer et éviter le stress, j'écoute de la musique ou je téléphone à un(e) ami(e).
> **(To relax and avoid stress, I listen to music or I telephone a friend.)**

Grammar

This is an appropriate topic in which to look at **GIVING ADVICE** in French.
The following are all used with the infinitive:

il faut	- it is necessary to / one must
tu dois	- you must
tu devrais	- you should
je te conseille de	- I advise you to
manger des légumes	- eat vegetables
boire de l'eau	- drink water
te coucher plus tôt	- go to bed earlier

and in the negative:

Il ne faut pas	- one must not
tu ne dois pas	- you must not
tu ne devrais pas	- you should not
je te conseille de ne pas	- I advise you not to
fumer	- smoke
boire de l'alcool	- drink alcohol
te coucher trop tard	- go to bed too late

Remember: after expressions of quantity de or d' is used:

beaucoup	- lots/many	beaucoup de fruits	- lots of fruit
trop	- too much/many	trop d'alcool	- too much alcohol
assez	- enough	assez de sommeil	- sufficient sleep

Mini Test

1. Give **5** piece of advice to a friend who needs to develop a healthier life-style!

Foundation

Qu'est-ce que tu penses du recyclage?
(What do you think of recycling?)
Je pense que c'est une bonne idée de conserver les ressources.
(I think it's a good idea to conserve resources.)

Quels sont les problèmes dans ton quartier?
(What are the problems in your area?)
Il y a beaucoup de circulation et ça pollue l'environnement.
(There's a lot of traffic and that pollutes the environment.)

A part ça, qu'est-ce qui te préoccupe?
(Apart from that what annoys you?)
Je m'inquiète des installations pour les handicapés aussi.
(I worry about facilities for the handicapped too.)

Comment peut-on améliorer la ville/le village?
(How can you improve the town/village?)
On a besoin de plus de magasins et il faut quelque chose pour les jeunes.
(We need more shops and something for the young people.)

Quel est le plus grand problème?
(What is the biggest problem?)
Pour moi, c'est les S.D.F.. Je trouve ça inquiétant.
(For me, it's the homeless. I find it worrying.)

RECYCLING CENTER

Est-ce qu'il y a d'autres problèmes?
(Are there any other problems?)
Oui, c'est très sale et il y a toujours des papiers par terre.
(Yes, it's very dirty and there is always litter on the ground.)

Vocabulary

l'environnement	- the environment		ça m'inquiète	- it worries me
les espaces verts	- green spaces		ça me choque	- it shocks me
la circulation	- traffic		ça m'embête	- it annoys me
la pollution	- pollution		ça m'énerve	- it irritates me
les déchets	- rubbish		ça me déplaît	- it displeases me
les inconvénients	- disadvantages		il manque de	- there's a lack of
les S.D.F. (Sans Domicile Fixe)	- the homeless		gâcher	- to spoil
le recyclage	- recycling		abîmer	- to ruin
l'élevage des animaux en batterie	- battery farming		conserver	- to conserve
la couche d'ozone	- the ozone layer		protéger	- to protect
le trou d'ozone	- the hole in the ozone layer		améliorer	- to improve
l'effet de serre	- the greenhouse effect		éviter	- to avoid
le chômage	- unemployment		gaspiller	- to waste

Higher

Et les pays du tiers-monde, est-ce que c'est notre responsabilité de les aider aussi?
(And what about the problems in the Third World, is it our responsibility to help them too?)
Je crois que nous serions très égoïstes de ne pas les aider seulement à cause de leur nationalité. Nous devrions toujours essayer de faire ce qu'il faut.
(I think that we would be very selfish not to help them just because of their nationality. We should always try to do what is necessary.)

Pour toi, quels sont les problèmes qui touchent notre société aujourd'hui?
(For you, what are the problems which affect our society today?)
A mon avis, le gouvernement devrait faire quelque chose pour aider les chômeurs.
(In my opinion, the government should do something to help the unemployed.)

Que penses-tu des problèmes de l'environnement comme, par exemple, le trou dans la couche d'ozone et l'effet de serre?
(What do you think of environmental problems such as the hole in the ozone layer and the greenhouse effect?)
Je pense que chacun devrait faire quelque chose pour aider si on veut améliorer la situation.
(I think that everyone should do something to help if we really want to improve the situation.)

Grammar

Verbs followed by an Infinitive

Some verbs are followed by a plain infinitive, others by de + infinitive and others by à + infinitive.

e.g. Je dois recycler   (I must recycle)
       J'ai décidé <u>de</u> recycler   (I have decided to recycle)
       J'ai commencé <u>à</u> recycler   (I have started to recycle)

You need to learn which verbs are followed by à, de or just an infinitive.

Here are a few useful ones:

+ infinitive

pouvoir	-	to be able (to)
vouloir	-	to want (to)
devoir	-	to have (to)
savoir	-	to know how (to)
aller	-	to go (to)
aimer	-	to like (to)
détester	-	to hate (to)
espérer	-	to hope (to)
compter	-	to intend (to)
il faut	-	it is necessary to

+ de + infinitive

cesser de	-	to stop (-ing)
décider de	-	to decide (to)
essayer de	-	to try (to)
éviter de	-	to avoid (-ing)
finir de	-	to finish (-ing)
avoir l'intention de	-	to intend (to)

+ à + infinitive

commencer à	-	to start (-ing)
aider à	-	to help (to)
se mettre à	-	to set to (-ing)
hésiter à	-	to hesitate (to)
s'amuser à	-	to have fun (-ing)
réussir à	-	to manage (to)/to succeed in

You will find the following phrases useful when conversing in French:

Pardon?	-	pardon/sorry?
Je ne comprends pas (très bien)	-	I don't understand (very well)
Pouvez-vous parler plus lentement?	-	Can you speak more slowly?
Pouvez-vous répéter?	-	Can you repeat?
épeler	-	spell
expliquer	-	explain
écrire ça, s'il vous plaît?	-	write that, please?
Ça s'écrit comment?	-	How is that spelt?
Je parle un peu/assez bien/bien/très bien le français	-	I speak French a little/quite well/well/very well
Je ne sais pas	-	I don't know
Vous me comprenez?/Tu me comprends?	-	Do you understand me?
Qu'est-ce que cela veut dire?	-	What does that mean?
Comment dit-on ... en anglais	-	How do you say ... in English
Comment dit-on ... en français	-	How do you say ... in French
Excusez-moi (vous form)/excuse-moi (tu form)	-	excuse me, I'm sorry
Je suis désolé(e)	-	I'm sorry
bonjour	-	hello, good morning, good afternoon
bonsoir	-	good evening
au revoir	-	goodbye
à bientôt	-	see you soon
à la prochaine	-	see you again
bonne nuit	-	good night
salut	-	informal greeting or farewell - hi, hello, bye, see you
ça va?	-	how are you?
oui, ça va bien, merci	-	fine, thanks
merci beaucoup	-	thank you very much
je vous/te remercie	-	thank you
je vous en prie	-	don't mention it
je t'en prie	-	don't mention it (informal)
de rien	-	don't mention it

The majority of instructions on your French exam papers will be in the target language. The following list is not exhaustive, but will help to illustrate the kind of instructions likely to be encountered.

vrai ou faux	-	true or false
Lisez	-	read
Regardez	-	look at
Trouvez	-	find
Écrivez (environ - mots)	-	write (approximately - words)
des phrases complètes	-	complete sentences
Décidez	-	decide
Identifiez	-	identify
Soulignez	-	underline
Encerclez	-	circle
Répondez (en français)	-	reply (in French)
Notez les détails	-	note the details
Mettez dans le bon ordre	-	put in the correct order
Faites correspondre	-	match up
Faites une liste	-	make a list
Faites une description	-	write a description
Faites une comparaison	-	write/make a comparison
Expliquez	-	explain
Mentionnez	-	mention
Pour chaque question	-	for each question
voici un exemple	-	here is an example
en chiffres	-	in figures/numbers
Répondez à toutes les questions	-	answer all questions
Vous n'aurez pas besoin de toutes les lettres	-	you will not need all the letters
Complétez/Remplissez	-	complete/fill in
la grille/le formulaire/les cases/les blancs	-	the table/the form/the boxes/the blanks
Cochez la case/la réponse correcte	-	tick the box/the correct answer
Choisissez la description qui correspond le mieux	-	chose the description which fits best

Specific to listening:

Écoutez	-	listen
Vous allez entendre (deux fois)	-	you will hear (twice)
Il y aura (deux) pauses	-	there will be (2) pauses

Specific to oral:

Saluez l'examinateur	-	greet the examiner
Parlez/Dites	-	speak/say
Posez des questions	-	ask questions
Présentez-vous	-	introduce yourself
Donnez/demandez les détails suivants	-	give/ask for the following details
Remerciez/finissez poliment la conversation	-	say thank you/politely end the conversation

Notes

You will normally be required to express yourself in two different ways:

a) in a situation that you might encounter while on holiday in the country - e.g. bank, shop, café

b) Talking about yourself.

Role Play

1.   Vous êtes à l'office de tourisme. Vous êtes le touriste. Votre professeur est l'employé. (i)

(You are at the tourist office. You are the tourist. Your teacher is the employee.)

   a.   Ask for some leaflets. (ii)

   b.   Ask for a list of hotels

   c.   Ask what time the banks close. (iii)

   d.   Say thank you and goodbye. (iv)

Role Play Notes

You are unlikely to know what this situation is until the day, but if you have revised well and learnt some stock phrases you should easily be able to cope. You will have some time to prepare.

(i)   Make sure that you appreciate where the situation is taking place (the Tourist Office), and who is who (you are the tourist). Also note the use of "vous" as this is a formal situation.

(ii)   Think what you actually need to say: ("I would like some leaflets"), remember you are unlikely to be able to look up "I would like" as it is part of a verb - this is where your memory comes in!

(iii)   Even if you can't manage to say the whole question, say what you can - even if it is just one or two words like "banque?", "fermé?", you never know, they may be the key words and may gain you points.

(iv)   Don't give up! Even if you feel you have not done your best on the rest of the conversation, make sure you finish it off. You will always get marks for communicating.

Conversation / Interview

a. Vous parlez avec la mère de votre correspondant(e). Elle vous pose des questions: (i);
    (You are talking to your penfriend's mother. She asks you some questions.)
    ou
    (or)

b. Vous avez un entretien pour un travail dans un bureau. Le patron vous pose des questions. (ii)
    (You have an interview for a job in an office. The boss asks you some questions.)

Personal details (iii)

Family (iv)

Hobbies and interests

School and daily routine

Future plans (v)

Work experience

Holidays (past/present/future) (vi)

Conversation / Interview Notes

All of these sections have been dealt with in this revision guide.
You do not want to waste valuable preparation time - make sure you are well prepared in advance.

(i)   Again make sure that you understand what you are being asked to do (answer your penfriend's mother's questions). Note the use of "vous". However, in this situation it may also be acceptable to use "tu" if you are struggling to remember the endings for "vous" as it is less formal and she may well have invited you to call her "tu".

(ii) This is a much more formal setting (an interview) and you are strongly recommended to use "vous".

(iii) Your teacher/examiner will prompt you with a question, try to give as much detail as possible and take the initiative to move on to talking about your family. Don't worry if you forget something, keep going, the more you say the better.

(iv) If you find yourself struggling or you are not sure what to say your teacher/examiner will pick up on this and will intervene with another question to help you. Aim to use a variety of vocabulary and different constructions throughout if you can. Also remember to try hard with your pronunciation and accent, even if it seems over the top to you!

(v)   This is where you are expected to bring in different tenses (if you haven't already done so). It's up to you whether you keep it simple and accurate or if you want to be a little bit more adventurous and original.

      Remember you do not have to tell the truth - no one will check! Have a look at the relevant sections of the guide for some ideas.

(vi) This is possibly the most demanding section as you may well be required to use a variety of tenses, try to keep cool and don't rush your answers, your teacher/examiner will help you if you get stuck.

The best preparation for this part of the GCSE assessment is to listen to as much spoken French as you can:

- Radio.

- Satellite television.

- A trip to France.

- Exchanging cassettes with a French penfriend.

- The use of listening materials from school.

Together with this, of course, you must have a sound base of French vocabulary across the topic areas. At Foundation Level you can expect to hear announcements, instructions, requests, dialogues, short news items. In fact there is a good deal of overlap between the vocabulary and phrases needed for the oral role-play situations and Foundation Level listening material. At Higher Level you can expect to hear longer and more complex passages. Some points to bear in mind for your listening exam:

- Before the exam, familiarise yourself with instructions in French (see page 71).

- Look carefully at any examples given.

- Always read the questions in advance so you know what you are listening out for

  e.g. question: il se lève à quelle heure <u>le samedi</u>?

You hear: Normalement, pendant la semaine, je me lève à sept heures moins le quart. Je me douche, je m'habille, je descends pour prendre le petit déjeuner et je quitte la maison à sept heures et demie. <u>Le samedi</u> je fais la grasse matinée - je ne me lève qu'<u>à neuf heures.</u>

Only the information underlined is required to answer the question. The rest can be ignored.

  Remember that you will hear the item more than once, and that you can make notes throughout.

- Do not worry, particularly at Higher Level, if you don't understand every single word. Again, concentrate on listening out for the information required by the question.

- Check how many marks a question is worth: if the whole question is worth 11 marks you know that you need to tick 11 boxes or provide 11 pieces of information.

- Check if answers have to be written in French or English. Remember that you do not have to answer in full sentences, and that French answers will not be marked for accuracy, only comprehension.

- If asked to tick 3 boxes, do not tick more than 3, in the hope that you may have the 3 correct answers amongst all your ticks! You will be penalised if you do this.

- Similarly, do not leave a question unanswered. There are no marks awarded for a blank space, but an intelligent guess may gain you marks.

The reading assessment is based on a range of written texts, varying in length and complexity from e.g. a short public notice to a magazine or newspaper article. Much of the advice for the listening exam is also relevant here.

- Read the titles and questions carefully. They often provide a helpful context.

- Scan the text for information related to the question, and then go back to the question - what exactly is wanted?

- Sometimes, especially with longer items, the trick is to understand the gist, the general idea, and not every single word.

- Sometimes it is a matter of finding the relevant bit of information in a longer passage, where you are not expected or required to understand everything.

- Sometimes the answer hinges on one little word, which you must be careful not to overlook, e.g.: Le musée est ouvert tous les jours sauf mardi.

Some candidates will read "tous les jours" (every day) and think they have found the answer regarding the museum's hours and days of opening, missing the vital word "sauf" (except). Make sure your revision includes a list of these short but very important words!

- Sometimes you will be expected to deduce meaning from the context, which may provide a clue:
"Le cèdre, un arbre très populaire"
"Un arbre" should help you realise the "cèdre" is a type of tree. From there, you should be able to see the similarity between "cèdre" and "cedar".

- Use clues offered by the language and grammar of the text; you will need to be able to recognise different tenses, singular and plural nouns and verbs, feminine and plural agreements, etc.

  e.g. the following words are provided for this gap-filling exercise:

  finir　lui　jeunes　sportive　tradition　arbre　écrire

  a. Les frères de Sophie sont plus _____ qu'elle.
  (adjective with masculine plural agreement required)

  b. C'est une _____ française (feminine noun required).

  c. Elle vient d' _____ (infinitive beginning with a vowel required following the construction "venir de" - to have just done something).

- Be aware of "faux amis" (false friends)
  e.g. "sensible" in French means sensitive, not sensible.

- Please read the section on the use of a French/English dictionary, in order to help you avoid the pitfalls (see page 81).

For specific details of the listening and reading assessments you will need to check the requirements of your own syllabus.

Foundation

You may be required to fill out a form or leave someone a note at Foundation Level:

A FORM

e.g. 1 - Vous avez perdu quelque chose. Remplissez le formulaire (i)

		marks
Date (ii)	le huit août	(1)
Nom/prénom (iii)	Smith Sylvia	(2)
Adresse	Hotel Paris, 40 rue de la Gare, Paris	(1)
Objet perdu	un sac à main	(1)
Description (iv)	grand, brun, en cuir, sale	(3)
Lieu (v)	à l'aéroport	(2)

Notes

(i)   As always, make sure you understand the instructions. Notice that they have left it up to you to decide what you have lost.

(ii) Try to include some French if you can rather than just putting the date in numbers.

(iii) Make sure you get your names the right way round!

(iv) This is your opportunity to include as much detail as possible. Check how many marks are available so that you can be sure to include enough information. Notice that it can be in note form rather than full sentences.

(v)   Remember to add the word for "at" or "in".

A NOTE

e.g. 2 - Tu sors avec un copain. Tu dois laisser un message pour ton correspondant pour lui dire où tu es allé, avec qui and à quelle heure tu reviens (i). Écrivez environ 25 mots (ii).

Marc,

Je suis allé au parc avec ton frère. Nous jouons au foot.

Je reviens à cinq heures.

David (iii)

Notes

(i) Once you have decided what you need to do, have a look at the instructions to see if there are any phrases you can use. You may need to change them around a bit.
e.g. Tu es allé (you have gone) - <u>Je suis</u> allé(e) (I have gone)

(ii) Notice how many words you need to write. This is never an exact amount but you may be penalised if your work is too short or too long; try to stay within 5 words either way on shorter tasks.

(iii) You should always check your work. A check list should include: spellings, genders, accents, agreements, verb endings, tenses

Higher

You may be required to write a letter to a friend, a formal letter or an article/essay.

A LETTER TO A FRIEND
e.g. 1 - Tu écris à ton correspondant pour décrire les vacances que tu viens de passer avec ta famille (i).
Écrivez environ 100 mots.

Milton Keynes, le 30 juillet (ii)

Chère Brigitte,(iii)

Je t'écris pour te (iv) raconter mes vacances à New York avec ma famille. Nous sommes (v) partis à 3 heures du matin et nous avons pris l'avion de Gatwick. C'est la première fois que j'ai volé et j'avais (vi) peur au début (vii), mais c'était (viii) super! Nous sommes restés dans un grand hôtel (ix) de 4 étoiles, je l'ai trouvé très impressionnant. J'ai mangé des burgers tous les jours, parce qu'ils sont (x) meilleurs là-bas qu'en Angleterre.

Qu'est-ce que (xi) tu fais cet été?

Écris-moi bientôt,

amitiés (xii)

Lisa

Notes

(i) Make sure you work out which tense you are being required to use (past tense here to describe holidays you've just been on), and whether the letter is formal (use vous) or informal (use tu).

(ii) Remember that in French you only need to head your letter with the place from which you are writing and the date.

(iii) Make sure you have an appropriate beginning (cher = "dear" for a boy, chère = for a girl).

(iv) You need an opening sentence to introduce the letter. Using indirect object pronouns (te) is impressive.

(v) Check your perfect tense, does the verb take avoir or être? If it takes être, does the past participle need to agree?

(vi) Using idioms such as "avoir peur" (to be afraid) shows that you have a good knowledge of the language.

(vii) Little time phrases like "au début" (at first) help to increase the variety of the vocabulary you use and to make your sentences more complex.

(viii) Give opinions wherever possible.

(ix) Use adjectives whenever you can; remember to check for agreements.

(x) Comparing things will also help to improve your marks for language.

(xi) Add a question, again it is a technique which will impress examiners.

(xii) Make sure that you finish with an appropriate ending such as "amitiés" (best wishes). Check that your letter is the right length. Check your work thoroughly (see note (iii) page 77).

A FORMAL LETTER

e.g. *2* - Vous écrivez à l'hôtel où vous êtes resté en vacances pour dire que vous n'étiez pas satisfait de l'état de la chambre (i). Écrivez environ 100 mots.

M. Jones J.

142 Church Street (ii)

Londres, le 21 août

Monsieur, (iii)

Je viens de retourner (iv) de mes vacances à Marseille où nous avons passé deux semaines formidables.

Malheureusement (v), mon copain et moi n'étions (vi) pas du tout satisfaits de la chambre à votre hôtel.

Il manquait (vii) des serviettes et (viii) il n'y avait jamais de savon dans la salle de bains. La fenêtre était cassée et la douche ne marchait pas. Aussi, les draps étaient sales et quand nous avons parlé à la femme à la réception, elle nous (ix) a dit "tant pis"!

Nous espérons recevoir un remboursement bientôt.

Je vous prie d'agréer, monsieur, l'expression de mes sentiments distingués (x).

J. Jones

Notes

(i)   Notice that you are required to write a formal letter of complaint (use vous) in the past tense; notice the use of the imperfect tense to describe the state of the room.

(ii)   You will need to give your full address as you expect a reply, notice how it is set out slightly differently.

(iii) Use Monsieur or Madame for a business letter to mean Dear Sir or Dear Madam.

(iv)   Again note the use of idiomatic expressions where the French is slightly different to the way we would phrase it in English.

(v)   Using adverbs is a nice touch.

(vi)   Be careful to check verb endings in instances such as these "my friend and I" = we.

(vii) Use the imperfect tense for description.

(viii) Try to use negatives other than NE ... PAS for more range of expressions.

(ix)   Again the use of indirect object pronouns shows that you can manipulate complex language.

(x)   It is worth learning a set phrase such as this for "yours sincerely/faithfully".

AN ARTICLE/ESSAY

e.g. *3* - Vous avez vu un concours dans un magazine français, le titre est "Les avantages et les inconvénients d'habiter dans une ville". Vous décidez d'écrire quelque chose (i). Écrivez environ 120 mots.

MA VILLE

J'habite dans une grande ville anglaise qui (ii) s'appelle Birmingham. Birmingham se trouve dans le centre de l'Angleterre et c'est une ville industrielle. J'y habite depuis (iii) seize ans - toute ma vie - et je l'adore.

Il y a beaucoup d'avantages si on habite une grande ville, c'est très vivant, il y a toujours quelque chose à faire et on a un grand choix de restaurants, de cinémas, de toutes sortes de choses.

Par contre (iv), il y a aussi des inconvénients. Par exemple (iv), il y a beaucoup de circulation et par conséquent (iv) beaucoup de pollution. C'est souvent très sale aussi parce que les gens laissent tomber leurs papiers par terre - ça m'énerve!

Mais malgré les inconvénients je préfère habiter en ville, peut-être parce que j'y suis habitué mais surtout à cause des opportunités qui existent là (v).

Notes

(i) You need to think about your layout and structure for an article such as this. Don't forget to give it a title - in French! If you have a title which asks you for the pros and cons of something you should try to give a balanced account. Normally you will need 4 short paragraphs (120 words isn't that much): an introduction, a paragraph for, a paragraph against and a conclusion where you decide which point of view you agree with.

(ii) Think about using a relative pronoun such as "qui" to link your sentences and make them more complex.

(iii) Using words such as "depuis" with the correct tense will gain you marks for grammatical accuracy.

(iv) These sort of linking words are common in an article of this type and are useful for bringing in counter arguments or to illustrate a point.

(v) Make sure that you back up your conclusion with a reason why; you should always be able to justify your opinions.

THE USE OF THE DICTIONARY

The use of a French/English dictionary for GCSE can be a mixed blessing. It can help with reading comprehension, and in the production of written French. You must, however, take care to learn words that you have looked up as you will not be allowed to use a dictionary during the exam.

You need to bear the following in mind when using your dictionary:

- Avoid the temptation to look up every single word.

- When alternative French words are offered in your dictionary, check each one in the French to English section to find the one with the correct meaning:

  e.g. English 'lead' – do you want ...

  ... plomb m. ?

  ... conduite f. ?

  ... direction f. ?

  ... laisse f. ?

  ...conduire?

  ... mener?

  ... dominer?

- Be aware that the different structures of French and English do not allow for word to word translation. You need a sound understanding of the rules of grammar and sentence structure.

- Be aware of words which are similar to English:

  e.g.   branch   -   branche

- Certain endings in English correspond to certain endings in French:

  e.g.   -y often equals -ie, e.g. economy   -   économie

                    -ly often equals -ment, e.g. completely   -   complètement

- Words which have a circumflex in French sometimes have an 's' in English:

  e.g.   forest   -   forêt

                    honest   -   honnête

- Words where dé in French is replaced by 'dis' in English:

  e.g.   discourage   -   décourager

                    disgust   -   dégoûter

Remember that your dictionary is not a substitute for a sound base of vocabulary or understanding of the rules of grammar and structure. Use your dictionary wisely and sparingly.

NOUNS

Nouns in French are either masculine (le) or feminine (la). When you look a word up in a dictionary "n.m." means "noun - masculine" and "n.f." means "noun - feminine".

e.g.
man - homme (n.m.)
woman - femme (n.f.)

PLURAL NOUNS

Plural nouns are usually formed by adding an "s" to the singular, unless the word already ends in "s", "x" or "z", in which case no change is made.

un homme - les hommes
un fils - les fils

Most nouns ending in -eau and -eu add an "x" in the plural:

e.g.
un gâteau - les gâteaux

Most nouns ending in -al change to -aux in the plural: e.g. un animal - des animaux.

NB: there are a number of irregular plurals in French. Some of these are:

le pneu - les pneus (tyres)
le chou - les choux (cabbages)
l'œil - les yeux (eyes)
Monsieur - Messieurs (gentlemen)
le grand-parent - les grands-parents (grandparents)
la pomme de terre - les pommes de terre (potatoes)

If unsure of the plural of a noun, check in your dictionary or grammar book.

DEFINITE ARTICLE

The definite article le, la, l', les is equivalent to the English "the":

e.g.
le garçon - the boy
la fille - the girl
l'homme - the man
l'avion - the aeroplane
les voitures - the cars

The definite article is used a lot more in French than in English:

e.g.
j'aime le chocolat - I like chocolate
C'est 80 cents le kilo - It's 80 cents a kilo
J'ai les cheveux blonds - I've got blond hair
Je parle (le) français - I speak French

INDEFINITE ARTICLE

The indefinite article un, une, des is equivalent to the English "a", "an" or "some":

e.g.
un éléphant - an elephant
une baleine - a whale
des dauphins - some dolphins

Omit the indefinite article when talking about jobs:

e.g.
il est avocat - he is a lawyer

À WITH DEFINITE ARTICLE

"à" combines with the definite article in the following way:

masc. sing	fem. sing	before vowel	plural
au	à la	à l'	aux

to mean "to", "at" or "in the":

e.g.　　je vais au café　-　I'm going to the café

　　　　je vais à l'église　-　I'm going to church

DE WITH DEFINITE ARTICLE

"de" combines with the definite article in the following way:

masc. sing	fem. sing	before vowel	plural
du	de la	de l'	des

to mean "of" or "from the ":

e.g.　　le garçon du café　-　the waiter from the café

THE PARTITIVE ARTICLE ("SOME")　　See page 45

ADJECTIVES

Adjectives and agreements, see page 11

In addition to adjectives met on page 11, adjectives which end in -eux, follow this pattern:

masc.	fem.	masc. pl.	fem. pl.	
délicieux	délicieuse	délicieux	délicieuses	(delicious)

Some adjectives double the last letter and add an "e" for the feminine:

gentil	gentille	gentils	gentilles	(kind)
gros	grosse	gros	grosses	(large, fat)
bon	bonne	bons	bonnes	(good, kind)

Many common adjectives are irregular; here are some of them:

blanc	blanche	blancs	blanches	(white)
long	longue	longs	longues	(long)
vieux (vieil*)	vieille	vieux	vieilles	(old)
nouveau (nouvel*)	nouvelle	nouveaux	nouvelles	(new)
beau (bel*)	belle	beaux	belles	(beautiful, handsome)
public	publique	publics	publiques	(public)
favori	favorite	favoris	favorites	(favorite)
léger	légère	légers	légères	(light)
cher	chère	chers	chères	(dear, expensive)
frais	fraîche	frais	fraîches	(fresh, cool)
fou	folle	fous	folles	(mad)
faux	fausse	faux	fausses	(false)

*vieil, nouvel and bel are used in front of masculine nouns which begin with a vowel or "h":

e.g.　　un vieil homme　-　an old man

　　　　un nouvel ami　-　a new friend

NB: when a feminine form of an adjective is given in brackets,
e.g.   travailleur(euse) - hardworking,
remember to remove the -eur from the masculine form and replace it with the feminine -euse to form
travailleuse.

POSSESSIVE ADJECTIVES

masc. sing (+fem. sing before vowel or "h")	fem. sing.	plural	
mon	ma	mes	(my)
ton	ta	tes	(your)
son	sa	ses	(his/her)
notre	notre	nos	(our)
votre	votre	vos	(your)
leur	leur	leurs	(their)

POSITION OF ADJECTIVES

In French the adjective is usually after the noun, e.g. les yeux bleus, un pantalon vert, but a number of very common adjectives are placed before the noun:

beau	-	beautiful, handsome
bon	-	good
grand	-	big, tall
gros	-	large, fat
haut	-	high, tall
jeune	-	young
joli	-	pretty
long	-	long
mauvais	-	bad
nouveau	-	new
petit	-	small
vieux	-	old
premier	-	first

e.g. une bonne idée - un jeune homme - une grande maison - le premier train

Sometimes the position of an adjective changes its meaning, as in the following examples:

la dernière semaine (des soldes)	-	the last week (of the sale)
la semaine dernière	-	last week
la prochaine fois	-	next time
l'année prochaine	-	next year
ma propre chambre	-	my own room
une maison propre	-	a clean house
ma chère amie	-	my dear friend
une voiture chère	-	an expensive car
mon pauvre frère	-	my poor, unfortunate brother
un homme pauvre	-	a poor man

COMPARATIVE AND SUPERLATIVE OF ADJECTIVES   see page 25

DEMONSTRATIVE ADJECTIVE   ce, cet, cette, ces, see page 47

INTERROGATIVE ADJECTIVE

meaning "what, which?"

masc. sing.	fem. sing.	masc. pl.	fem. pl.
quel	quelle	quels	quelles

e.g. Tu as lu ce livre? - Quel livre?

Have you read this book? - Which book?

TOUT

masc.	fem.	masc. pl.	fem. pl.
tout	toute	tous	toutes

e.g. Toute la famille était là - the whole family was there.

Je fais du sport tous les jours - I do some sport every day.

ADVERBS

You will find an explanation of how to form an adverb on page 61. Adverbs are INVARIABLE with the exception of tout (all, very, quite, altogether) which maintains its adjectival forms (tout, toute, tous, toutes).

e.g. il est tout près d'ici (it's very near here)

elle est toute fière de son frère (she is very proud of her brother)

COMPARATIVE AND SUPERLATIVE OF ADVERBS

e.g. Le saumon coûte cher. (salmon costs a lot)

To make a comparison you need to use "plus" (more) or "moins" (less) before the adverb and "que" (than) after it.

e.g. Le champagne coûte plus cher que le saumon (Champagne costs more than salmon).

Le saumon coûte moins cher que le champagne (Salmon costs less than champagne).

Superlatives need "le plus" or "le moins" before the adverb:

e.g. Le caviar coûte le plus cher (Caviar costs the most).

Le pain coûte le moins cher (Bread costs the least).

Note these irregular forms:

bien (well)	mieux (better)	le mieux (best)
mal (badly)	plus mal (worse)	le plus mal (worst)
beaucoup (a lot)	plus (more)	le plus (most)
peu (little)	moins (less)	le moins (least)

VERBS

INFINITIVES

Remember these will end in either -ER, -RE or -IR. This determines their endings in the present tense (see pages 13 & 15).
Irregular verbs such as avoir (see page 9) must be learnt as they do not conform to these patterns.

For verbs followed by an infinitive, see page 69.

Some adjectives are on occasions followed by à + an infinitive.

e.g. premier (first)
     Il était le premier à partir (he was the first to leave)
     prêt
     Prêt à porter (ready to wear)

also note
beaucoup (lots), e.g. beaucoup de choses à voir (lots of things to see)
rien (nothing) , e.g. rien à manger (nothing to eat)

Apart from EN + present participle (see page 65), the infinitive is the only verb form which can follow a preposition: à, pour, sans, avant.

e.g. pour finir (in order to finish)
     sans dire au revoir (without saying goodbye)
     avant de quitter la maison (before leaving the house)

For explanation of FAIRE + infinitive, see page 53.

TENSES

Verbs in French have different endings and forms depending on the subject of the verb, (je, tu, il, elle, on, nous, vous, ils, elles) and the tenses.

PRESENT TENSE

Examples of regular -ER, -RE and -IR verbs in the present tense are given on pages 13 and 15.
Some -ER verbs with spelling changes in the present tense are:

(1)
acheter	-	to buy			
j'achète	-	I buy	nous achetons	-	we buy
tu achètes	-	you buy	vous achetez	-	you buy
il/elle achète	-	he/she buys	ils/elles achètent	-	they buy

Also, (se) lever, mener, peser, se promener

(2)
manger	-	to eat			
je mange	-	I eat	nous mangeons	-	we eat
tu manges	-	you eat	vous mangez	-	you eat
il/elle mange	-	he/she/eats	ils/elles mangent	-	they eat

Extra "e" in nous form keeps the "g" soft. Also changer, nager, partager.

Note also the following example where "c" becomes "ç" in the "nous" form, to keep the "c" soft in front of the letter "o":

je commence	-	I start	nous commençons	-	we start

(3)
essayer	-	to try			
j'ess**ai**e	-	I try	nous essayons	-	we try
tu ess**ai**es	-	you try	vous essayez	-	you try
il/elle ess**ai**e	-	he/she trys	ils/elles ess**ai**ent	-	they try

Also nettoyer, payer, s'ennuyer

(4)
jeter	-	to throw			
je je**tt**e	-	I throw	nous jetons	-	we throw
tu je**tt**es	-	you throw	vous jetez	-	you throw
il/elle je**tt**e	-	he/she throws	ils/elles je**tt**ent	-	they throw

Also (s') appeler

IRREGULAR VERBS

A number of very common verbs in French are irregular, i.e. they do not follow the normal pattern. The present tense of avoir, être, aller, faire and the four modal verbs (pouvoir, vouloir, devoir and savoir) can be found in the guide on pages 9, 15, 31 and 41 respectively. A good dictionary or grammar reference will provide an irregular verb table.

REFLEXIVE VERBS

- present tense, see page 19
- perfect tense, see page 63

Note also the following uses of reflexive verbs:

La porte s'ouvre/se ferme	-	the door opens/closes
Ce livre se vend partout	-	this book is on sale everywhere
Ça se voit	-	that is obvious (can be seen)

Some common reflexive verbs other than those connected with daily routine on page 19 are:

se trouver	-	to be found
s'arrêter	-	to stop
s'asseoir	-	to sit down
s'étonner	-	to be surprised
se sentir	-	to feel (emotion, etc.)
se plaindre	-	to complain
se marier	-	to get married
se dépêcher	-	to hurry
se fâcher	-	to be angry
se reposer	-	to rest
se promener	-	to go for a walk
se souvenir de	-	to remember

THE IMPERATIVE - COMMANDS

See page 39, for "tu" and "vous" forms
In the "nous" form the imperative is translated by "let's ...",
e.g. allons-y! Let's go! Chantons! Let's sing!

Again, this is formed by taking the nous form of the present tense:
nous allons, nous chantons and removing the "nous".

THE PERFECT TENSE

- with avoir, see page 29

Some common irregular past participles (other than those met on page 29)

past participle

avoir (to have)	-	j'ai eu	- I had, have had, did have
boire (to drink)	-	j'ai bu	- I drank, have drunk, did drink
comprendre (to understand)	-	j'ai compris	- I (have) understood, did understand
dire (to say)	-	j'ai dit	- I (have) said, did say
être (to be)	-	j'ai été	- I was, have been
lire (to read)	-	j'ai lu	- I (have) read, did read
mettre (to put)	-	j'ai mis	- I (have) put, did put
pouvoir (to be able to)	-	j'ai pu	- I was able, have been able to
savoir (to know how to)	-	j'ai su	- I knew, have known, did know
voir (to see)	-	j'ai vu	- I saw, have seen, did see
vouloir (to want to)	-	j'ai voulu	- I (have) wanted, did want to

PRECEDING DIRECT OBJECT

With "avoir" verbs, the past participle does not change to agree with the subject. However, if there is a direct object (noun or pronoun) which precedes the verb, THE PAST PARTICIPLE MUST AGREE WITH THE DIRECT OBJECT.

e.g.   J'aime tes chaussures. Où est-ce que tu les as achetées?

"e" and "s" added to past participle "acheté" to agree with "chaussures" (feminine plural).

For more examples, see page 49.

PERFECT TENSE WITH ÊTRE   See page 33

Verbs which take être in the perfect tense:

past participle

aller (to go)	-	allé	
venir (to come)	-	venu	- also devenir (to become) revenir (to come back)
arriver (to arrive)	-	arrivé	
partir (to leave)	-	parti	- also repartir (to set off again)
entrer (to go in)	-	entré	- also rentrer (to go back in, return)
sortir (to go out)	-	sorti	
monter (to go up)	-	monté	- also remonter (to go up again)
descendre (to go down)	-	descendu	- also redescendre (to go down again)
rester (to stay)	-	resté	
retourner (to return)	-	retourné	
tomber (to fall)	-	tombé	
naître (to be born)	-	né	
mourir (to die)	-	mort	

sortir, monter, descendre and rentrer can be used with avoir in the perfect tense with an object and have a different meaning:

elle a sorti son porte-monnaie de son sac   - she took her purse out of her bag

elle a monté les valises   - she took the suitcases upstairs

REFLEXIVE VERBS IN THE PERFECT TENSE See page 63

APRÈS AVOIR, APRÈS ÊTRE + PAST PARTICIPLE

Note the following structure which in English means "having done something":

après avoir mangé, j'ai fait
la vaisselle — having eaten, I washed up

après être rentrée, elle a écrit
une lettre — having returned home, she wrote a letter.

Note that in the second example, the past participle "rentrée" agrees with the feminine subject because it is a verb which takes être in the perfect tense.

THE PLUPERFECT TENSE

The perfect tense is used when talking about something that has happened in the past. The pluperfect tense goes further back in time and expresses something that HAD happened prior to an action already in the past.

J'avais déjà mangé quand un ami a téléphoné pour m'inviter au restaurant.
I had already eaten when a friend telephoned to invite me out to the restaurant.

The pluperfect is formed in a similar way to the perfect tense, with a past participle and part of avoir or être; but with the pluperfect it is the IMPERFECT of avoir or être which is used.
Il était déjà parti quand je suis arrivé(e). He had already left when I arrived.

THE IMPERFECT TENSE

Another past tense. It describes something that used to happen regularly in the past.
e.g. Quand j'étais jeune, j'allais à la patinoire tous les samedis
When I was young, I used to go ice-skating every Saturday.

It is also used for description, particular of the weather and other prevailing conditions.
It is often translated in English by "was/were ... ing".
Pendant les vacances, il faisait beau tous les jours. (During the holidays, the weather was fine every day.)
Il faisait du brouillard, alors je n'ai pas vu le cycliste. It was foggy, so I didn't see the cyclist.
See pages 32 and 43.

THE CONDITIONAL See page 37.

THE FUTURE

(i) aller + infinitive to express the future. See page 27.
(ii) the future tense. See pages 27 and 28.

EN + PRESENT PARTICIPLE See page 65

THE NEGATIVE   See page 23

In addition to those forms of the negative given on page 23, note also the following:

ne ... nulle part - nowhere - je <u>ne</u> le vois <u>nulle part</u> - I can't see him anywhere

ne ... ni ... ni ... - neither ... nor - je <u>n</u>'aime <u>ni</u> le poisson ni les frites - I don't like fish or chips

ne ... aucun(e) - no - Je <u>n</u>'ai <u>aucune</u> idée - I have no idea

As aucun(e) is an adjective, it must agree with the noun which follows.

Some further points regarding word order with the negative:

- If the verb being made negative is an infinitive, both parts of the negative precede the infinitive:

    e.g. Il a décidé de ne pas sortir - He decided not to go out.

- Pas, rien, personne, jamais, aucun(e) can be used on their own without "ne":

    e.g. Tu as déjà visité la France? Jamais (never)

    e.g. Qui as-tu vu en ville? Personne (no-one)

- ne ... personne, ne ... que, ne ... nulle part are slightly different in the perfect tense in that the second part of the negative comes <u>after</u> the past participle: je <u>n</u>'ai vu <u>personne</u> (I saw no-one)

Remember that after a negative "<u>de</u>" is used and not du/de la/ de l'/des: Je n'ai plus <u>de</u> chocolat!

PREPOSITIONS

These indicate place, position or location. Some can be used in more than one way therefore it is best to note meanings and examples as you come across them.

e.g.

<u>à</u> - à Paris - to/in Paris

- <u>au</u> marché - to the/at the market (see page 83.)

- à pied - on foot

- <u>au</u> deuxième étage - on the second floor

- à vingt kilomètres - 20km away

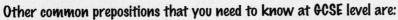

Other common prepositions that you need to know at GCSE level are:

après	-	after
avant	-	before
avec	-	with
chez	-	at (the house of)
dans	-	in, inside
de	-	from, of
depuis	-	since, for (+ period of time)
dès	-	from (a specific moment in time)
e.g. dès sa naissance	-	since his birth
en	-	in, of, by, to (see note page 51)
jusque	-	as far as, until
par	-	by, through, per
pendant	-	during, for
pour	-	for, in order to
sans	-	without
sous	-	under
au-dessous de	-	beneath
au-dessus de	-	above, over
sur	-	on, over
vers	-	to, towards, about

PRONOUNS

Pronouns are words which replace nouns to save you from repeating yourself.

e.g. Isabelle mange le gâteau - elle le mange.

(Isabelle is eating the cake - she is eating it.)

There are many different types of pronouns, some of which have been dealt with in sections throughout the guide.

SUBJECT PRONOUNS

je	- I	nous	- we
tu	- you	vous	- you
il	- he	ils	- they
elle	- she	elles	- they

These replace names or nouns to tell you who is doing the action of the sentence.

e.g. Maman fait le ménage - Elle le fait.

(Mum is doing the housework - she is doing it.)

DIRECT OBJECT PRONOUNS

See note on page 35 for present tense and position.
See note on page 57 for perfect tense and negation.

INDIRECT OBJECT PRONOUNS   See note on page 49.

When used in positive commands these need to come after the verb.

e.g.   Demande-lui! (ask him!)

In these circumstances, as with direct object pronouns "me" and "te" change to "moi" and "toi".

e.g.   Demande-moi (ask me)

Some verbs require an indirect object, here are some common ones:

montrer à	- to show (to)
téléphoner à	- to telephone
donner à	- to give (to)
offrir à	- to offer (to)
envoyer à	- to send (to)
dire à	- to say (to)
répondre à	- to reply (to)
écrire à	- to write (to)
demander à	- to ask
promettre à	- to promise

e.g. Je téléphone à ma tante - je lui téléphone
(I phone my aunt - I phone her.)

EN AND Y   See note on page 59

STRESSED/EMPHATIC PRONOUNS   See note on page 17

These are also used when a pronoun stands on its own.
e.g. Qui veut venir? Moi!
    (Who wants to come? Me!)

Also after c'est or ce sont:
e.g. Qui est-ce? C'est moi
    (Who is it? It's me!)

You can also add "seul" or "-même" to the pronoun:
Lui seul sait le faire.   Je vais le faire moi-même.
(Only he knows how to do it.)   (I'm going to do it myself.)

You also need to use them when there are two subjects to the verb and one or both of them are pronouns.
e.g Mon frère et <u>moi</u> jouons au tennis. (My brother and <u>I</u> play tennis.)

Also as the second part of a comparison.
e.g. Je suis plus beau que <u>lui</u>. (I'm better looking than <u>him</u>.)

LEQUEL – INTERROGATIVE PRONOUN

Lequel, laquelle, lesquels, lesquelles must agree with the noun that they stand for and are used to mean "which one(s)?".
e.g. Laquelle des jumelles a gagné le concours?
    (Which of the female twins won the competition?)

Relative clauses involving a preposition.
After a preposition where you need to distinguish between people and things, use "qui" for people.
e.g. Le garçon <u>avec</u> <u>qui</u> je sortais.
    (The boy with whom I was going out.)

Use lequel, laquelle, lesquels, lesquelles for things:
e.g. Le stylo <u>avec</u> <u>lequel</u> j'écrivais.
    (The pen with which I was writing.)

Note the following changes:
      à + lequel   -   auquel
   à + lesquel(le)s   -   auxquel(le)s
     de + lequel   -   duquel
  de + lequel(le)s   -   desquel(le)s

e.g. Le marché auquel nous allons.
    (The market to which we are going.)

Quite often "où" may be used to replace "dans lequel" or "sur lequel":
e.g. Le lit sur lequel je couchais   -   Le lit où je couchais.
(The bed on which I was lying   -   The bed where I was lying.)

USE OF "QUOI?" (INTERROGATIVE PRONOUN)

This can be used on its own.

e.g. Je veux te parler de quelque chose. - Quoi?
(I want to talk to you about something. What?)

Or after a preposition.

e.g. À quoi ça sert? (What's the use of that?)

or as an exclamation.

e.g. Il est mort. - Quoi!
(He died. What!)

or in set expressions

e.g. Quoi de neuf? (What's new?)

POSSESSIVE PRONOUNS

Singular Masc Fem		Plural Masc Fem	
le mien/la mienne	mine	les miens/les miennes	mine
le tien/la tienne	yours	les tiens/les tiennes	yours
le sien/la sienne	his/hers	les siens/les siennes	his/hers
le/la nôtre	ours	les nôtres	ours
le/la vôtre	yours	les vôtres	yours
le/la leur	theirs	les leurs	theirs

e.g. C'est ma clé, tu as perdu la tienne.
(It's my key, you've lost yours.)
Voilà ton pull, tu as vu le sien?
(Here's your jumper, have you seen his?)

The pronoun must agree with the object owned NOT the owner.

e.g. J'ai mon appareil photo mais Lise n'a pas le sien.
(I've got my camera, but Lise hasn't got hers.)

Note that "le sien" means "hers" in this case, because it is describing a masculine object (un appareil photo) belonging to a girl.

You can also use à + stressed pronouns (moi, toi, etc.) with être to denote ownership.

e.g. à qui est ce pull? C'est à moi.
(Whose is this jumper? It's mine.)

Il est à moi.   Elle est à toi.
(It's mine)   (It's yours)
Ils sont à lui.   Elles sont à nous.
(They're his)   (They're ours.)

RELATIVE PRONOUNS

See note on page **55** for use of "qui" and "que".

Ce qui and ce que/ce qu' are used when there is no other antecedent.

(i.e. does not refer back to a specific object/idea)

e.g. Ce que j'aime c'est ...

   (What I like is ...)

   Ce qui me plaît c'est ...

   (The thing that pleases me is ...)

DONT

"dont" means "whose" or "of which". It is used for persons, animals and things.

e.g. Le garçon dont je connais le frère.

   (The boy whose brother I know.)

CELUI, CELLE, CEUX, CELLES

See note on page 47.

CECI AND CELA

These represent an idea rather than a noun and mean "this" and "that" respectively.

eg. Il est très intelligent.   Cela m'étonnerait!

   (He is very intelligent.   That (the idea of it) would surprise me!)

Cela is often shortened to "ça".